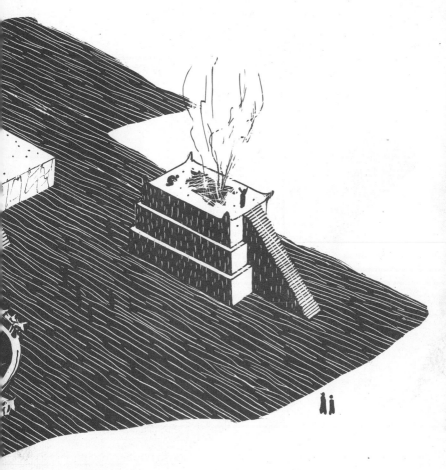

SOLOMON'S TEMPLE

The Way It Was
IN BIBLE TIMES

by
MERRILL T. GILBERTSON

illustrated by
THOMAS E. MAILS

VERITAS OMNIA VINCIT

AUGSBURG PUBLISHING HOUSE
Minneapolis, Minnesota

Auspices, Board of Christian Education
of The Evangelical Lutheran Church

This little book is

dedicated to

Olga,

my

co-partner in the Lord.

PREFACE

It was the author's privilege to study at the Biblical Seminary in New York, where concentrated, inductive study of the Bible opened new vistas of enjoyment, appreciation, and comprehension of the Scriptures. The Bible became alive; the characters moved from one page into another, bringing the promise and plan of God's redemption in Christ from Genesis to Revelation. This systematic study of the Scripture instilled a vivid curiosity about the background of the Bible land people used by God to bring His great salvation to men. For eight years the author, through the inspiration of his many students at Waldorf College, continued this interest in Bible backgrounds. During these years, books on archaeology, Bible geographies, Bible histories, travelogues of Palestine, and source books for Bible backgrounds, became friendly companions on reading expeditions.

In 1951, the author was privileged, through a gift from Bethel, Immanuel, and Our Savior's churches of Joplin and Chester, Montana, to spend a summer traveling in the Holy Land, walking the trails and paths of Jesus. This created an ever-deepening realization that the land, the climate, and the geographical location of the country accounted for the habits, customs, manners, and employment of the interesting folks who had lived in Bible times. The ruins of their cities, the artifacts of the museums and libraries, the modern excavations, all poured forth evidences of their background.

In the spring of 1956, the author prepared a thesis in partial fulfillment of the requirements for the degree, Master of Religious Education, at the Biblical Seminary. As a result of this thesis, the manuscript for this book, *The Way It Was,* became a reality. Grateful acknowledgement must be made to Dr. Emily J. Werner of the Biblical Seminary who spent many long hours in guidance during the writing of this thesis. She proved to be a helpful friend and counselor in every way. Without her encouragement this book would not have been possible.

Grateful acknowledgement must be made by the author to his wife Olga Coltvet Gilbertson for her inspiration and encouragement in the study of Bible backgrounds, for her helpfulness in literary construction, and for her painstaking care in proofreading this little book. Deep appreciation must be expressed to Professor Kenneth Hanson of Iowa State Teachers' College, Cedar Falls, Iowa, to Miss Evelyn Wolf of Waldorf College, Forest City, Iowa, and to Mrs. Morris Sorenson of Albert Lea, Minnesota, for their painstaking care in stenographic work involved in this manuscript.

CONTENTS

INTRODUCTION

One of the common complaints about the Bible is that it is difficult to understand. Others maintain that much of the Scriptures is meaningless or even misleading. This unjust criticism of God's Holy Word comes because the reader does not know the background or setting of the material it contains.

For example, why did Jesus seem to feel that Simon the Pharisee had slighted his guest by not washing his feet, anointing his head, or greeting him with a kiss (Luke 7:44-46)? To the modern reader these seem to be most unnecessary if not annoying actions on the part of a host. But in the days of Jesus these were customary evidences of hospitality and respect.

Or again, it may seem odd to us that the Baby Jesus was wrapped in swaddling cloths. Why did the shepherd boy gird his loins? Why was bread always broken instead of cut with a knife? Why was the washing of the hands a religious ceremony? These things are confusing or meaningless in our present day. Yet, a study of the backgrounds of these Bible land people reveals that these customs were meaningful and necessary to them.

An understanding of the times in which the Bible was written is necessary for an appreciation of its true meaning. This is especially true today. The rapid and revolutionary changes taking place on every hand are making people conscious of an urgent need of something solid and unchanging to which they may cling. The problem of instability is baffling to young and old alike. Where shall we turn for security? Wherein lies the secret of the calm inner life? Where is the Rock upon which to build our houses?

There is only one Rock foundation upon which to build, and this is the Word of God. But, tragically, the average person does not have sufficient understanding of the Bible and its message to stabilize his fluctuating and fluttering spiritual life. How can we get a greater insight into the Word to understand its message better?

This is an eye-minded age. People think in pictures. Television, cinema, picture magazines, and other visual means of communication have trained the minds of young and old to be pictorially minded. People remember what is seen and presented in a graphic way. This eye-mindedness is definitely needed in the study of God's Holy Word. Its writers avoided discussions of abstract ideas. They used concrete, picture-filled language which abounded with illustrations and descriptions which would be common to the experiences of the people of their day. We need insights into their life to throw light on what all this imagery means.

The Bible was written 19 centuries or more ago by Oriental people, in an Oriental setting. The writers used Oriental modes of thought. It is easy for people who have spent their entire lives in the Western world to overlook these facts. A common error of most Bible readers is to put into the Scriptures Western manners and customs instead of interpreting them from the Eastern point of view. Many passages that are difficult to understand

are readily explained by a knowledge of the customs of
the Bible land. In fact, it is impossible to really understand the Scriptures unless one knows something of the
way these Oriental people lived! A. Hovey in his book,
The Bible, emphasizes this when he says:

A study of the Bible backgrounds will render an inestimable
service to Christianity, not only by confirming the truth of the
Bible in many ways, but also by rendering it more intelligible
to the popular mind.*

Most people do not have enough background information to make the Bible live. The Bible must come out
of the life of its people in Bible times and enter into the
life of the reader in our present day. But it must be
understood in its own age before it can be applied to our
times. Because of this, the study of historical and physical
backgrounds, settings, customs, and culture is very important to an understanding of the Bible's real meaning
and purpose. A thorough understanding of the mental,
physical, and spiritual background of these people will
serve as a means of comprehending the message they
present.

The pages of the Bible will no longer present fruitless
frustrations if we are prepared to meet its characters on
the very ground on which they stood, in the homes
where they lived, and at the tables from which they ate.
Most of us feel distant, cool, and ill at ease among
strangers. People become friends when we know them
well enough to understand their emotions of joy, fear,
sorrow, peace, anxiety, and contentment. The more in-
timately we get to know folks the more we can appreciate what they say, do, think, and believe. For this
reason it is extremely important that the reader of the
Bible be familiar with its people, times, and customs.

What is a millstone? a potsherd? a mattock? a sheep-

─────
*Hovey, Alvah, *The Bible* (Griffeth and Rowland, Philadelphia),
p. 43.

fold? How did these people make a living? What kind of clothing did they wear? What sort of foods did they eat? What were their homes like? These are a few of the questions that constantly confront the reader of God's Holy Word.

The Bible begins with these words, "In the beginning . . ." This goes back indefinitely. To comprehend events in the life of Adam, Noah, Abraham, Moses, Isaiah, Amos, or John the Baptist, one must turn back millions of pages of history.

For an understanding of the lives of these people, we are dependent on the Bible itself, and other books written during Bible times. However, in the past 20 years we have been given insights into the life of Bible land people such as men have never known before. It was an interesting providence of God that the cradle of the Bible should have been placed in arid, sandy regions of the world. Humid, torrid jungles would have rotted away the telltale details of these ancient Hebrews. But in Palestine, silt and sand have sealed their tombs, preserved their relics, and protected their treasures. We can hold in our hands their pottery, lamps, knives, millstones, ornaments, and images. Even their modes of writing, art designs, mathematics, contracts, and trade transactions have been preserved on tablets of clay and stone for us. Only sand and silt could have performed such a wonderful service for posterity.

Trained and skilled archaeologists have spent long hours digging painstakingly among the ruins of ancient cities and civilizations. Because of these discoveries, we can now determine the culture of this people, reproduce their homes and furnishings, and ascertain their mode of living.

All of this helps us to become better acquainted with the message of the Bible. It opens for us a new understanding and appreciation of the Word. Digging into the past brings to light insights that kindle our imagination and make us anxious to study the Scriptures.

Transformed lives come only as the Holy Spirit enlightens and sanctifies us through the reading, studying, and hearing of the Word. To be ignorant of the Word is to close the door in God's face. Dare we then, through lack of appreciation, go into our Bible reading and become discouraged because we are on a foreign soil, in a strange home, and among unfamiliar folks? Let us not miss the message of salvation that God has for us because we have failed to utilize the light available to us from an understanding of the past.

This book has been written as an attempt to share with our people the Bible backgrounds necessary to appreciate and grasp the real significance of God's message of salvation to men through Jesus. Great care has been taken to eliminate unfamiliar terms and expressions. Every item treated has been carefully selected because of its relevance to a deeper understanding of God's redemptive plan.

It has been written especially for those who study the Bible in their home, and for the Sunday school teachers who share the Word. May these Bible backgrounds deepen the enjoyment, appreciation, and understanding of the Scriptures.

TENT OF HAIR

CHAPTER ONE

Houses
of
Hair

Home to the early Israelite was where he pitched his tent. Until sometime after the Hebrews had established themselves in Canaan following the sojourn in Egypt, they were a nomadic people. They did not settle down in cities, but moved from place to place to meet the forage requirements of their livestock. Naturally their houses were easily portable tents.

Tents are mentioned as dwelling places as early as Genesis 4:20, where Jabal is described as the "father of those who dwell in tents." Abraham "pitched his tent" near Bethel (Gen. 12:8). Isaac encamped in the valley of Gerar (Gen. 26:17); Jacob, near Shechem (Gen. 33:18).

What an imposing array the tent villages of Abraham must have made on the fields of Canaan! When Lot was taken captive by the kings of Elam, Shinar, and Ellasar, Abraham went out after them with 300 trained men born within his household. How many hundreds of tents it required for such a family must be left to the imagina-

tion. These encampments of tents were arranged in
circles for defense purposes.

During the 40 years of wandering in the wilderness,
God's chosen people were tent dwellers. Moses said,
"The people of Israel shall pitch their tents by their
companies, every man by his own camp" (Num. 1:52).
For many years after they entered the Promised Land,
they still lived in tents. Even in the days of King David
many of the people lived in this type of home. Jeremiah
wrote, "The whole land is laid waste: suddenly my tents
are destroyed" (Jer. 4:20).

Truly, the tent of the Israelite was his home. How
simply and interestingly these tents were made! Women
of the household wove all the material for these "houses
of hair" on a family loom. And they were literally made
of hair. Coarse black goat's hair was woven into strips
of varying width, depending on the size of the hand
loom. These strips were in turn sewed together to make
a tent of the desired proportions. Its dimensions varied
with the number of individuals making up the household. The average tent stretched fifteen feet long and ten
feet wide.

During the first heavy rains the goat hair shrank,
making the material almost waterproof. This heavy
material protected the family from the cold in the winter. During the summer the flaps of the tent were lifted
to form a sunshade. Solomon gives an interesting picture
of these tents in his song, "I am very dark, but comely,
O daughters of Jerusalem, like the tents of Kedar" (Song
of Solomon 1:5).

A look inside one of these tents would have disclosed
a curtain hanging from the middle of the roof to separate
the women's quarters from those of the men. Thus Sarah
at Mamre, in her compartment, overheard the conversa-
tion between Abraham and the angel (Gen. 18:10). In
many families the men and women had separate tents.

In Genesis 31:33 a reference is made to the tent of Jacob, to Leah's tent, to Rachel's tent, and to the tent of the two maidservants.

These tents were very flexible. As the family increased in size they added another few feet to the length of the tent. This is the background of Isaiah's plea, "Enlarge the place of your tent, and let the curtains of your habitations be stretched out; hold not back, lengthen your cords and strengthen your stakes" (Isa. 54:2).

Nine poles, arranged in rows of three, supported the roof of the tent. The middle three were six or seven feet high; the others ran parallel along the front and back. The tent was stretched taut by long ropes or cords. These cords held the poles in position, and tent pegs fastened the tent to the ground.

This "house of hair" was an emblem of the Israelites' simple, unfettered life. How these people loved the out-of-doors and really preferred the tent to the house of wood and stone which came into use later! The Apostle Paul was the most famous maker of tents in Scripture.

Tent Furnishings

We have taken a look at the tent structure. Now let us lift up the flap and observe the furnishings. Everything was extremely simple. The floor was hard-packed earth. Among poorer families there was no floor covering of any kind. However in the more progressive homes,

PALLETS

**GOATSKIN
BAG**

the occupants used mats of straw or wool or coarse camel hair rugs.

Along the sides of the tent bed rolls or pallets were piled in tiers. A collection of pots, pans, kettles, and the caldron hung from the wooden post. Over against one pole were the goatskin bags and bottles. The family pestle and mortar stood near the door. (Num. 11:8). Every home had a kneading trough (Ex. 12:34). No habitation was complete without the millstones (Deut. 24:6). The tent lamp stood on a stand. For those who were fortunate enough to have a camel, the saddle bag served as a seat (Gen. 31:34).

All of this household equipment could be packed at a moment's notice and carried by the women or placed on the back of a camel in case of an attack or a decision to move to better pastures. The making, pitching, and taking down of the tent was wholly the women's job. They became experts in staking out an encampment. The women made their own stoves for baking the bread and cooking the family food by simply setting up a few stones at the tent door. They heated these stones with charcoal until they were warm enough to bake the flat cakes of bread.

The House of Brick and Stone

The progress of a people is often observed in the improvements they make in their homes. During the reign of King David, the people gradually changed from their nomadic ways and began to settle down to carry on farming. This necessitated building more permanent homes. One by one the "houses of hair" began to disappear, and homes of mud, brick, and stone became the accepted thing.

The Hebrews were still an outdoor people, so they did not at first build large homes. They preferred the freedom of the out-of-doors. All they desired of a home was shelter. The women were usually out in the fields working with the men. Hence, the house served principally as a place to eat and sleep.

The Israelites built the walls of a house from unbaked mud and clay bricks which were dried in the sun. Sometimes they made the corners of stone so as to support the roof beams. Soon they discovered that houses of hair and clay were vulnerable to attack by robbers and enemies. As Job said, "In the dark they dig through houses" (Job 24:16a).

Consequently they began to make more permanent homes of stone. This introduced the art of stonecutting and masonry. Sandstone was very common in the land and was readily available for the construction of this new type of house. These stones were not always cut, so they often varied a great deal in size. Mortar made of mud held the stones together. They built these small one-room houses in villages.

In the cities the people built larger and better homes. Here they preferred to have more than one room. However, they did not build the rooms side by side as we think of a home today. They divided a two-room home by a space or open court. If the home consisted of three or four rooms, it was built around a central court. The length of the court depended upon the number of rooms planned. The front of the rooms faced the court because each family wanted to be a closely-knit unit.

The courtyard was open to the sky. Here they planted trees, shrubs, and flowers for beautification. Every court had its cistern to catch rain water and to serve as a

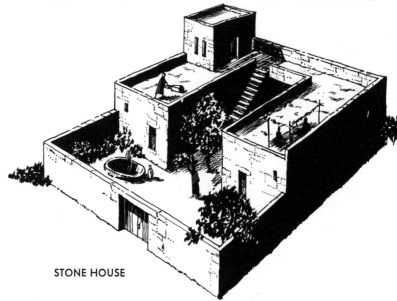

STONE HOUSE

storage place for the limited water supply. In a cistern like this Jonathan and Ahimaz hid from Absalom. A woman covered the top of the well with ground grain so that the men were not found (II Sam. 17:18-19).

Floors

Even in larger homes with several rooms these simple folk had no floor except the dirt upon which the house was built. The ground was made smooth and packed firmly. Sometimes lime was mixed into mud and spread over the floor until it hardened. This type of floor could be swept and was comparatively dust free. In some cases cobblestones and shale were mixed with lime and packed into the floor. The best covering for a floor consisted of large square slabs of limestone laid end to end. This was permanent, and could be scrubbed. At the time of Christ, the Romans introduced mosaic floors. These were made by embedding small, smoothly-cut squares of stone into the wet earth. In homes of the wealthy the floor was paved with marble and ornamented with bands of black slate and colored stone.

Roofs

The roof of these larger homes was supported by several large, roughly dressed logs which were laid across from wall to wall. Smaller beams were laid at right angles with the large timbers. Above these beams was placed a layer of thin boards. This in turn was covered with reeds, grass, thorns, or mats of straw. Over this surface the builder spread about ten inches of wet earth and clay; all of this was tramped down and packed very tightly. A large stone roller smoothened the surface. Finally a layer of sand and pebbles was scattered on top. After every rain the roof was rolled and repacked to prevent leakage. Every roof had its stone roller, stored in one corner for future use.

With clay roofs we can easily visualize green grass growing during the rainy season. The Psalmist says, "Let them be like the grass on the housetops, which withers before it grows up" (Psalms 129:6). Isaiah spoke of his people as being like the "grass on the housetops" (Isa. 37:27).

The homes of the wealthy were covered with tiles of baked clay that could easily be removed and repaired. Thus the four friends of the palsied man were able to carry him up the outside stairway to the rooftop, remove the tiles, and lower him so that Jesus might speak those immortal words, "My son, your sins are forgiven" (Mark 2:3-5).

The roof was supported from the inside by one or more

pillars rising from the center of the room to strengthen the crossbeams. When the Philistines gathered in the temple of Dagon to rejoice over the capture of their enemy, Samson, these center pillars played an important part (Judg. 16:29).

The Outside Stairs and Housetop

On the outside of the houses, whether of the poor or the wealthy, people built stairs that led to the roof. These stairs were made of stone. Much of the family life was enjoyed on the housetop, especially in the cool of the evening. The streets were dusty and noisy, while on the roof it was quiet and restful. Solomon preferred a little corner of his roof to a wide house with a contentious woman (Prov. 25:24).

Peter, in the house of Simon the Tanner at Joppa, went up on the housetop to pray (Acts 10:9). Grain, fruits, and fuel were spread out on the housetop to dry in the hot sun. When Joshua's spies came to Jericho in Canaan, Rahab hid them under the flax that she had spread out on the roof to dry, and in so doing saved their lives (Josh. 2:6). In the summer, the entire family would leave the close confinement of the lower quarters to go up on the housetop to sleep. In large houses and palaces great groups of people often gathered on the housetop.

Palestinian roofs were used in so many ways that it was necessary to have laws requiring the owner of the home to build a parapet or railing around the rooftop in order that neighbors and friends might not fall off and injure themselves (Deut. 22:8).

The Upper Chamber

Every family longed for an upper chamber or enclosed room on the housetop. Those who were unable to afford

ROOFTOP
BOOTH

this luxury had to satisfy themselves with a booth or shelter of palm leaves, straw, or reeds upon the roof so that they too might have, in a small way, an upper room.

The more prominent folk built this upper room of wood or stone. It served as a cool place of retreat from the confusion of the household animals, traders, and beggars on the narrow streets below. When guests were in the home it served as a place of hospitality. The Shunamite woman and her husband built such a room for Elisha "and put there for him a bed, a table, a chair, and a lamp" so that he might have a place to stay (II Kings 4:10). It was in such an upper chamber that Jesus instituted the Lord's Supper. The disciples met together in an upper room after the Ascension to wait the coming of the Holy Spirit. If more than one room was built on the roof, it was sometimes called a summer house (Amos 3:15).

Windows

The homes, whether large or small, had few windows. The openings toward the street were usually located high in the wall as a safety measure from intruders. Large windows opened into the courtyard. Glass for windows was unknown, so the large openings were barred with wood or covered with a frame of lattice work. The psalmist was probably thinking of these open, latticed windows when he said, "Even the sparrow finds a home, and the swallow a nest for herself, where she may lay her young, at thy altars, O Lord of hosts" (Ps. 84:3). At night the windows were closed with shutters for privacy and safety. The windows in the upper rooms would not need bars as no thief could scale the walls.

Doors

The doorway was a place of peculiar sanctity and importance. The difference between the outside of the home and the inside was that of two distinct worlds. The inside was a haven of shelter, where noise, confusion, and intrusion were shut out. The outside was an impersonal place, filled with thieves and enemies. In larger homes a doorkeeper sat at the entrance to answer inquiries for the family and to admit guests. At night he slept in a little room near the door. In the smaller village home this responsibility was shared by the members of the family. The father's place of importance was at the door.

The doors were left open all day as a symbol of hospitality. A closed door signified that the family had done something of which they were ashamed. At sunset the door was closed and remained so until the next morning. This accounts for the parable that Jesus told of the person whose friend refused to give him three loaves of bread at midnight. He was told, "Do not bother me; the door is now shut, and my children are with me in bed; I cannot get up and give you anything" (Luke 11:5-7). Ancient locks were made of wood, as were the keys to the doors. Ordinarily the doors were made of sycamore wood. Only the wealthy ornamented their doors with cedar.

Furnishings of the Stone House

The furnishings of the simple one-room dwelling were slightly different from those of the tent. In the city home, a shelf displayed the cooking utensils of copper. Piles of bedding and pallets were stored in a recess of the wall. These later developed into clothes closets.

Around three sides of the wall were divans or couches, covered with cotton, wool, silk, or gilded cloth from the native looms. It was the custom to sit on the divan during the day with the legs crossed. At night the divan became a bed. Some were very elaborate. Amos spoke of beds of ivory (Amos 6:4).

A large brass brazier in the center of the room gave warmth and a cheerful glow to the home. The peasant's dining table was a wicker mat, but for the rich a large brass tray was brought into the room and set upon a carved stand. Rugs and carpets of every hue covered the floors of the rich.

BRAZIER

OIL
LAMPS

The Lamp

Light was supplied by an olive oil clay lamp set on a stand whence "it gives light to all in the house" (Matt. 5:15). The Palestinian dreaded and abhorred the dark, for night was the time of danger from robbers, hostile neighbors, and the enemy. It was only men of evil who loved the darkness (John 3:20). Thus the lamp was very precious to the householder.

The cheapest type of lamp was little more than a saucer, with a lip at one end where the wick rested. When the Greeks invaded Palestine, they introduced a more elaborate type of lamp. This was closed at the top and had a hole at one end from which the wick emerged, and a lip at the other end into which oil was poured. The top of the lamp was often impressed in an elaborate pattern of flowers and leaves. Sometimes a handle was added. Taste and ingenuity varied the shape and ornamentation. Solomon's lamps for the temple were of gold (I Kings 7:49).

The lamp burned all night even in the poorest homes. The ideal woman (Prov. 31:18) never allowed her lamp to go out. When the oil was low, the lamp gave off an offensive odor and smoke. This was an indication that the oil had to be replenished. If the wick was well worn, the housewife would quench the fire and put in a new wick. The wick was often made of twisted strands of cotton or flax. This was put into the saucer of oil.

Lampstands were not in use during Old Testament times. However, during the days of Jesus, they were common. Archaeologists have found many of these lampstands. Some were made of bronze, 14 or 16 inches in height. The poor no doubt had a less expensive type. If the family could not afford a stand, the lamp was placed in a niche in the wall or on a bushel that had been turned upside down. If the family had a table, this too served as a place to set the lamp.

In the King James version of the Bible the words "candle" and "candlestick" were used. This was because candles were in such common usage at that time in England. Actually, the folks of Bible times knew nothing of candles. A literal translation of the word is a lamp or light, not a candle.

The Inn

Because of the rigid laws of hospitality among the Hebrew people, inns were not a necessity. Abraham and the other patriarchs were so conscious of the difficulties and dangers of traveling that they considered it a sacred duty to offer any traveler a place of refuge in their own homes. Travelers were dependent upon this hospitality of the natives for their lodging at night. If the family had an upper room, this would be turned over to the traveler.

The first mention of an inn is in the story of the return of Jacob's sons from their visit with Joseph in Egypt (Gen. 42:27). This lodging place was located in Egypt. The inns of Palestine were probably established much later, as there is little allusion to them in the Old Testament.

Whatever inns they had were located close to watering places and were probably just camping grounds. The people had to provide their own food, cooking utensils, and other provisions for sleeping and living. At important points where the caravans traveled, these inns were sometimes more elaborate. Here the traveler might purchase food and provisions.

The inn was probably just a large empty room where men and cattle were housed together.

CHAPTER TWO

Breaking Bread

OVEN

Bread and water would probably not represent starvation fare to the person of Bible times. On the contrary, it would be more likely to suggest abundance, or at least an adequate supply of food. Bread and water were the two essentials of life (Isa. 3:1). In the arid lands of the Near East, a sufficient supply of water was a constant concern. If you had this and bread you could live. The term bread often stood for food in general. Famine was described as a time when there was no bread (Amos 4:6). Prosperity was a time of fullness of bread (Prov. 20:13).

Bread

Since it was considered so essential—truly their staff of life—these people had an attitude of reverence toward bread. They would never cut bread with a knife, for that would be to cut life itself. Therefore, bread was always broken before being distributed to those partaking of the meal. Thus, "Jesus took bread, and blessed, and broke it, and gave it to the disciples" (Matt. 26:26).

The expression "breaking bread" was also used to describe eating an entire meal, including whatever food might be served with the bread. So Luke wrote, "On the first day of the week, when we were gathered together to break bread, Paul talked with them" (Acts 20:7).

Much of the housewife's time was spent in making this food. The wheat, brought from the threshing floor, was separated from bits of stone, earth, straw, and weeds. This wheat was sifted carefully (Luke 22:31b). Afterwards the grain was washed and spread out to dry on sheets of skin or cloth, on the housetop or in the open court below. The clean, dry grain was then stored in the kitchen in large churn-like barrels or vessels made of wicker or clay. Some homes had underground cisterns or pits to store the wheat.

To make flour, the grain was usually pounded with a pestle and stone mortar (Lev. 2:14) or ground in a hand mill. The mill was made of two circular stones, 18 to 24 inches in diameter. The upper stone was rotated by hand on the lower one. The lower stone was convex and made of limestone or basalt. In its center was a pivot which projected through a hole in the middle of the upper stone. The hole was larger than the pivot.

The women poured the grain, a handful at a time, through this hole into the mill. From the upper stone extended a wooden peg which they could grasp to revolve the mill. The larger mills were elevated so that a donkey, fastened to a singletree, would turn the stones.

MILL

The size and weight of this stone was illustrated by
Jesus very forcefully in the story of the millstone
(Mark 9:42). These mills produced the flour for bread.

For unleavened bread the flour was mixed with water
and salt in a wooden or baked clay kneading bowl.
The dough was made into flat cakes for baking, usually
12 to 16 inches in diameter and from one-eighth to

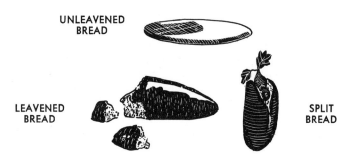

UNLEAVENED
BREAD

LEAVENED
BREAD

SPLIT
BREAD

one-quarter of an inch thick. People ate unleavened
bread in connection with their feasts or in time of
dire need. It was an indication of bread baked in a
hurry. Lot served this to his unexpected guests (Gen.
19:3). The Jews ate it at the Feast of the Passover as
a remembrance of their oppression and suffering in
Egypt, and their haste in leaving. Unleavened bread was
also symbolic in that it was free from the corruption
or fermentation of yeast.

Leavened bread was made by adding to the dough a
lump of leaven saved from the previous baking. Yeast
or wine lees were used to cause the fermentation. The
batter stood until the entire mass had been leavened,
usually overnight. Early in the morning this dough was
mixed with more flour, water, and salt, and again set
aside until the dough was raised.

Another interesting bread was cut about six inches

in diameter. In the baking process the heat separated the loaf into an upper and lower layer of bread, hollow in the middle. In this loaf the workman would carry olives, figs, and dates, as if in a bag.

A third kind of bread was a small loaf similar to a biscuit. It was this kind that the lad gave to Jesus during the miracle of the feeding of the 5,000 men. Parched wheat, made of immature heads of wheat roasted to a dark color, formed a substantial food for these people (Ruth 2:14). The raw grain too was often eaten. The disciples of Jesus plucked the ears of grain, rubbed them between their hands, and ate them (Luke 6:1).

"Corn" as we know it today was not grown in Palestine. When corn is referred to in the Bible, it indicates either wheat, barley, millet, or spelt. Pharaoh's dream of seven ears of corn on one stalk refers to seven heads of grain on one stalk (Gen. 41:22). These grains were ground into flour for bread. Wheat flour was no doubt preferred, but was expensive; coarse barley or millet loaves were the staple diet of the peasants.

To bake the bread a fire was built on a flat stone. When the stone was thoroughly heated, the embers were raked off and the cake of dough laid on it. To bake the other side this same process was repeated with the cake turned over. Hosea used this imagery when he said, "Ephraim is a cake not turned" (Hos. 7:8).

Later, bread was baked over a convex sheet of iron, supported on stones six or eight inches above the ground. A fire of thorns or small brush burned underneath this to heat the iron. In the city, bread was sent to a public oven to be baked. This oven was shared with several of the neighboring families and the women had to wait for their turn. Here at the oven, the women sat and chatted, plying their needle work or embroidery as they waited for the bread to be baked. These public ovens were domed stone huts, fire being built underneath.

Manna

God provided a unique kind of bread for the Israelites
in the wilderness by giving them manna every morning,
except on the Sabbath day. Every Friday a double portion was collected (Exod. 16:4-5). It came in the form
of small, round seeds resembling hoarfrost (Exod. 16:
14). It had to be gathered early, before the sun rose,
to prevent melting. If one gathered more than was
needed, the manna would become wormy and spoiled.
It was prepared for food by grinding and baking. When
they arrived in Canaan other food was plentiful so
God no longer provided it. Manna was a miraculous gift
of food from God.

Water

The melting snows of Lebanon and Mount Hermon
sank into the ground, to burst forth at various places
in springs or fountains which watered the thirsty land
of Palestine. From these waters came the Sea of Galilee
and the Jordan River. In certain places wells were dug
into the ground until an underground stream was tapped.
Jacob's well in Samaria was a good example of this
(John 4:6). In other places it was necessary to dig
cisterns to catch rain water. If these should become dry
from delayed rains or if the cistern became cracked
(Jer. 2:13), a water famine would ensue (Jer. 14:3). At
such time water would be sold in the streets by the
measure.

Water was carried to the house in large clay pots,
supported and balanced on the heads of the women of
the household. The pitchers or jars were very gracefully
made in long cylindrical forms. Some of the water pots
had two handles while the cheaper types had only one.
Only the women used the earthenware pots to carry
water. No wonder the disciples could easily locate the

upper room where the Passover was to be kept. It
would be a rare occasion to
find a man carrying a jar of
water (Mark 14:13-16).

WATER PITCHERS

The day's supply of wa-
ter was always carried at
twilight, in the cool of the
evening. Thus the woman
of Samaria betrayed her un-
popularity with the other
women by coming to the
well at noontime (John 4:
6-7). The women brought with them to the well a
long rope and a leather bucket in order to reach
the water at the bottom of the well. With this leather
bucket they filled the clay pot. The woman of Samaria
carried this equipment with her to the well, but Jesus
did not have any way to draw water. No wonder she said
to Him, "You have nothing to draw with, and the well
is deep" (John 4:11). The women loved to stand by the
wells and fountains to visit and gossip about the day's
adventure.

A small earthen pitcher of water was kept standing
on the window sill during the day, where the water was
kept cool through the process of evaporation by the
breeze. At night this pitcher stood by the head of the
bed.

No village or city could be built where there was no
supply of water. Often large cities had only one source
for the entire community. The people learned to love
the taste of the water from the city fountain. When he
was a fugitive, David longed for water from the well
at Bethlehem (II Sam. 23:15). When a large amount
of water was to be carried, the men used large skins of
goats or sheep to carry it.

Oil

Oil played an important part in the diet of Bible land
people. They obtained it by crushing olives in a large
stone mill. They used the bulk of the olive crop for this
purpose. The oil was stored in clay or bronze jars,
or it might be put in cemented cisterns beneath the
ground. Oil was essential in the preparation of certain
foods and usually took the place of butter and animal
fat. The widow complained to Elijah that she had only
a little oil in the cruse. She could not prepare a meal
without it (I Kings 17:12).

Milk

The tent dwellers lived on a very simple fare. Since
there was little settled agriculture to begin with, the
Israelites depended largely on their domestic animals
and the little herbage that grew wild for food. Ready-
made food was the milk of goats, ewes, and camels, preferred in that order. In the intense heat of this climate,
milk had to be used at once or boiled.

To make butter, cream was poured into a goatskin
bag and rocked against the knee until butter formed.
This then was melted and boiled, the impurities skimmed
from the surface, and the butter stored for later use.

Cheese was also a popular food (I Sam. 17:18). The
most common food made of milk was "leben" or curds,
which was the residue of a soured milk (Prov. 30:33).
This was probably what Jael served to Sisera (Judg.
5:25). Abraham treated his guests to curds, milk, and
flesh of a young calf (Gen. 18:7-8). These people con-
sumed a great deal of sour milk as they felt it quenched
the thirst better in this form.

Honey

God promised the Israelites that He would lead them to a land "flowing with milk and honey" (Exod. 3:8). This must have been music to the ears of the hungry and thirsty wanderers in the wilderness. The numerous references to honey in Scripture indicate that Palestine must have abounded in this product.

Most of the references imply that wild honey was very common. The bees built their hives in the hollows of trees. Here Jonathan found honey (I Sam. 14:25-27). Honey was also found in clefts of rocks (Ps. 81:16). Samson ate honey from the dried carcass of a lion (Judg. 14:8-9). John the Baptist lived on locusts and wild honey (Matt. 3:4).

Often poems of the Old Testament use honey as an illustration. The ordinances of God's Word are compared to honey (Ps. 19:10). The bride's speech, in Solomon's Song, is like honey (Song of Sol. 4:11). Pleasant words are likened to honey (Prov. 16:24); wisdom is called honey for the soul (Prov. 24:13-14).

Meat

Meat was not usual fare at an Israelite meal. It was expensive, and few people could afford to eat it. On rare occasions they ate the flesh of bullocks, lambs, and kids. Sometimes these were roasted whole, and so thoroughly done that the meat would readily fall off the bones.

For very special guests, or if a special sacrifice was to be made to God (Amos 5:22), the "fatted calf" was killed. This calf was kept in a stall or pen, and given all the food it could possibly eat so as always to be ready for butchering. The fatted calf was not killed until the special guest arrived. Then it was "quickly" prepared and served as a delicacy.

When the witch of Endor entertained King Saul with a meal, she killed the fatted calf and "quickly" prepared it for her king and his servants (I Sam. 28:24-25). Abraham "quickly" prepared a calf for the three men who came to his tent to foretell the birth of a son (Gen. 18:7-8).

When the father welcomed home the prodigal son he said to his servants, "Bring 'quickly' the best robe and put it on him; and put a ring on his hand, and shoes on his feet; and bring the fatted calf and kill it and let us eat and make merry" (Luke 15:22).

Game such as venison was eaten if available. Other game such as ducks, geese, partridge, harts, gazelles, and roebucks were eaten.

God's people were forbidden to eat the flesh of animals that chew the cud and do not have a split hoof. This meant that camels, rabbits, and hogs were never used as food. The eagle, falcon, raven, ostrich, sea gull, hawk, vulture, stork, and heron could not be eaten either. Nor was any creature of the water to be eaten that did not have fins and scales (Lev. 11:1-47).

Meat was boiled or roasted on hot stones. Generally it was cooked with herbs and vegetables into a type of stew. Meat was always served in the container in which it was cooked.

Fish was abundant and cheap near the Mediterranean Sea and the Sea of Galilee. It was usually boiled over coals. They also learned to salt the fish so it could be kept longer. Fowl, such as quail, pigeons, and partridges were roasted whole.

Sometime between the days of Elijah and the birth of Christ the domestic fowl and the everyday use of eggs was introduced into Palestine. Jesus spoke of a son asking his father for an egg (Luke 11:12).

The locust is mentioned as part of the diet of John the Baptist. We are not sure how the Hebrews served locusts. An old Assyrian drawing shows locusts threaded on a skewer, ready to be brought into a feast. Sometimes the legs and wings were picked off and the bodies roasted, dried, salted, or ground up with flour and baked.

Agricultural Foods

The Hebrews also depended upon foods which were products of the earth, wherever they could be found. In an oasis, moisture and heat helped to produce dates. Figs and grapes could be cultivated. The fruit of the vine was made into wine, which could be kept without refrigeration in this hot climate.

The drinking of wine was almost universal. It was made locally and was cheap and plentiful. Water fit to drink was always at a premium except near the Sea of Galilee. During the six months of the year when there was no rain, water became very scarce. However, wine could be preserved and kept available at all times. The sediment of wine was called "lees." Jeremiah speaks of this, "Moab . . . has settled on his lees; he has not been emptied from vessel to vessel" (Jer. 48:11).

Olives cured in strong brine were a regular part of the diet. Sometimes the olives were cracked to hurry the curing process, otherwise it was necessary to wait several months after harvest before olives could be eaten with meals. Raisins were in common use (I Sam. 25:18); pomegranates were also eaten (Deut. 8:8).

Anise and mint were used as seasonings. The Hebrews seemed to enjoy strong flavors. They used coriander and black cummin to take the place of pepper. No stew would be considered palatable without these two flavors. Spices were imported from the East. Ointments, salves, oils, and creams of every description were used for protection against sunburn, flies, fleas, and vermin. Those who could afford it used sweet spices and aromatic gums imported from Arabia to cover up offensive odors.

The cucumber was in common use at this time (Num. 11:5). Melons, leeks (similar to chives but eaten as a green), garlic, and onions were a part of the menu. The pulse that Daniel and his friends longed for in their Babylonian captivity was probably a vegetable dish of Palestine (Dan. 1:12). Jacob used lentils in his famous red stew (Gen. 25:34). The lentil is smaller than a pea. It can be made into flour for bread or put in soups and stews. The red lentil was favored above the white variety.

The Significance of Eating

Eating and drinking together among the people of Bible lands signified a bond of friendship that was highly respected. When they ate together, there was bread and salt (Num. 18:19) between them and they were no longer strangers to each other, no matter what their previous relationship might have been. Bread and salt were the two most important items of food. To share them was to forget all previous grievances. This made eating almost a sacred affair.

In keeping with this, the Israelites were forbidden to eat with Gentiles. To do so would cause uncleanness. They could not touch a Gentile or anything handled by these unclean people. Thus all social contact with Gentiles was forbidden.

CHAPTER THREE

PRAYER SHAWL

Your
Cloak
Also

The kind of clothing worn by Bible land people was determined largely by the climate and the outdoor life they lived. The primitive nomads wore garments made of the skins of their flocks and herds. These served as protection from the rainy season and the cold winds.

The development of spinning, weaving, and embroidery brought many changes. The people discovered that loose garments permitted the circulation of air. On cool nights and during winter weather, heavier clothes kept out the elements. A cloth over the head protected the scalp from the rays of the burning Palestinian sun. Sandals soothed the feet of the weary travelers.

The dress of the poor was always simple. The advance of culture and an improved economy added color and design to the clothing worn by the merchant and artisan.

31

The Tunic

The important item of clothing was the tunic. This was a long kimono-like garment worn next to the skin. It was made of leather, haircloth, wool, linen, or cotton. Women wore them as well as men. These were often made without sleeves and reached to the knees. The wealthier people had sleeves in their tunics. Among the poorer classes of people the tunic was often the only garment that was worn in warm weather. People of higher rank used the tunic in the privacy of their homes, but they never appeared in public without an outer garment.

In the Bible the word "naked" is often used of men who wore only their tunic (Isa. 20:2). When Jesus sent out the disciples on their internship He told them not to take more than one tunic with them (Matt. 10:10). Sometimes in the Bible this word has been translated "coat," which really gives the wrong connotation. It was, however, correctly referred to as a linen garment (Lev. 6:10), or a linen cloth (Mark 14:51).

The Coat

Several garments were worn over this tunic. The simplest one was called a coat. Joseph's coat of many colors was a garment like this (Gen. 37:3). This was similar to the tunic except that it always had sleeves. The sleeves of the coat had long pointed ends which reached almost to the ground. These points were very convenient when a person was working, for he could tie them together and throw them over the shoulders, leaving his arms free. The action of baring the arms is an indication of readiness for energetic action (Isa. 52:10).

The Cloak

The cloak is often mentioned in Scripture. This garment was also called the robe or mantle. It was similar to the coat in many respects, yet it was a looser and longer kind of garment. It had no sleeves and was not held together by a girdle as were the tunic and the coat.

The tearing of the robe was a symbol of horror. With both hands the robe was ripped at least a handbreadth to indicate that now everything was ruined and torn asunder. When Job heard of the loss of his oxen, sheep, camels, and children, he rent his robe (Job 1:20). Caiaphas tore his robe at the trial of Christ when he accused Jesus of blasphemy (Matt. 26:65).

Hannah made a little robe and brought it to her son every year (I Sam. 2:19). David, upon finding King Saul in the cave, cut off a part of the king's robe (I Sam. 24:4). Elijah used his cloak to strike the waters of the

TUNIC AND GIRDLE   COAT   CLOAK

Jordan when he crossed over with Elisha. When Elijah
went into heaven, his robe became the property of Elisha
(II Kings 2:13). The three young men cast into the
fiery furnace were clad in their mantles or cloaks (Dan.
3:21).

The robe was made by sewing together two lengths
of thick woolen material. In some cases this garment was
woven without a seam. This was true of the one Jesus
wore (John 19:23). Because of the size and weight of
this robe, it also served as a blanket or coverlet for the
evening. The shepherds had no other blanket or covering. Travelers found these robes very convenient as they
slept out-of-doors.

The Girdle

The tunic was held close to the body by the girdle.
Ordinarily this girdle was just a broad leather belt,
usually six inches in width and fastened either in a knot,
by twisting it around itself, or with a clasp. This was
the kind of girdle worn by Elijah (II Kings 1:8), and
by John the Baptist (Matt. 3:4). Those who loved fine
clothing had girdles made of broad bands of silk, linen,
or heavily-embroidered material. The girdle was often
used to fasten a sword to a man's body (I Sam. 25:13).
It was also used as a purse in which to keep money.
Sometimes food was carried in the girdle, and the ink
horn of the scribe was kept there.

When Jesus said to His disciples, "Let your loins be
girded about," He simply meant that they should pick
up the long loose ends of their cloak and tuck them in
under the girdle so that they would be free to run or
move swiftly. It was not easy to run after sheep or wild
animals with these long flowing robes. Thus in Bible
language the phrase "to be girded" means to be ready
for action, to be free to move swiftly.

Paul spoke of the girdle as a necessary part of the Christian's armor in the fight against sin. Paul knew that the entire armor of the Roman soldier was held in place by the girdle, thus he proclaimed that the Christian armor should be held in place by the girdle of truth (Eph. 6:14).

Sandals

Sandals were the common footwear of Bible times. They consisted of a sole of either leather or wood which was fastened to the foot by leather thongs (Gen. 14:23). More often than not the toes were left uncovered. In some cases, however, there might be a covering for most of the foot. In walking over the dusty roads of Palestine the people paused often to shake off the dust from their feet. They did this by removing the sandal and slapping it against a stone or a wall.

Socks or stockings had no part in the dress of Oriental people. Because they trod in the dirt and dust of the roads, people always removed their sandals on entering a house, or any sacred place. It was the task of the humblest servant to wash the dust from the feet of one who came from a journey. John the Baptist felt that he was not even worthy to perform the task of untying the sandal, let alone washing the feet, of Jesus. In comparison to Jesus, he was lower than the lowest servant (John 1:26-27). Jesus was willing to serve in this capacity by washing the disciples' feet (John 13:3-5).

Because of their contact with various forms of disease and filth, sandals were a sign of degradation (Ps. 108:9), of abasement (John 1:27), or of despising a right. The next of kin to Ruth gave up his right to walk on the fields of Naomi by drawing off his sandal and giving it to Boaz (Ruth 4:7-8).

The Turban

When in public, the Hebrews
always wore a turban. The intense heat of the summer sun
made it dangerous to expose one-
self to its direct rays. The turban
was made of thick material
wrapped around the head several
times. Job spoke of the turban
(Job 29:14). Isaiah said that the
turban was one of the signs of
finery worn by the people. The
turban and girdle were often the
most ornamental parts of men's clothing.

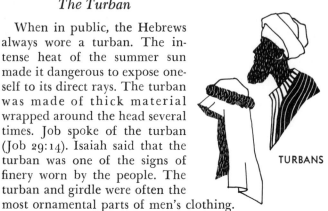

TURBANS

The shepherds preferred a head cloth to a turban as
it was cooler and afforded more freedom to catch move-
ments of the breeze. This head cloth was kept in place by
a black coil of camel's hair.

The Hebrew people gave much attention to their hair.
They loved to wear it long and were proud of their
thick, heavy, curled hair (II Sam. 14:25-26). The men
sometimes trimmed their hair a little. Only once are
barbers mentioned in the Old Testament (Ezek. 5:1),
but razors are often referred to. The men were very
proud of their long beards. The beard was a mark of
manly dignity. Little is known about the hairdress of
the women except that some used braids (I Tim. 2:9).

The Dress of Women

The law of Moses forbade men to wear women's
clothing or women to dress like men (Deut. 22:5). The
difference in the dress of the two was in detail rather
than the kind of clothing. The women wore the tunic
as an undergarment, the coat as a dress, and the cloak
for warmth, but they used colored needle work of black,

yellow, red, and green silk to give a feminine touch. Sometimes their outer cloak was made of silk. Thus these robes would often indicate distinctions of social rank. The women's garments were longer than those worn by the men.

The veil was the distinctive apparel of the women. All women wore veils, except maidservants and immoral women. Normally they never laid them aside, except when they were only in the presence of their servants or were alone in their quarters. Thus Rebekah, when she saw Isaac approaching her camel caravan, covered her face with her veil (Gen. 24:64-65).

The Prayer Shawl

Jewish men and boys wore a prayer shawl when they went to the synagogue on the Sabbath. This was always worn by the orthodox Jew when he was observing the hours of prayer. It was a large oblong cloth, three feet wide and five feet long, made of fine material, often in broad black and white stripes. At each corner of the prayer shawl hung a tassel of eight threads, twisted together in five knots. The law prescribed the type and color of the thread to be used and the way the thread was to be twisted and the number of knots permitted. The shawl was carried over the arm on the way to the synagogue. In the building itself, the shawl was placed over the head and shoulders.

The Phylactery

The phylactery was a strip of parchment upon which were written, with a special ink, four passages of Scripture. These passages were:

Ex.	13:2-10	Deut.	6:4-9
	13:11-17		11:13-22

These parchments were rolled up in a case of black calfskin which was attached to a heavier piece of leather and worn on the left arm at the elbow. Phylacteries were also worn on the forehead. These phylacteries were written on four strips and put into four tiny cells in a square case. This case was fastened to the forehead by a band around the head. The Pharisees probably wore these at all times, while the ordinary people wore them only during times of prayer. Women were not permitted to wear them. At the age of 13 the boys began to wear the phylactery. Jesus rebuked the Pharisees for their hypocrisy in broadening their phylacteries so as to be seen of men. (Matt. 23:5).

Ornamentation

The men often carried a cane or a staff. These varied in design from a plain stick of wood to those that were hand carved and highly ornamented at the top. This cane served as a support while walking and as a protection from wild animals and robbers.

Men also wore a ring (Luke 15:22), which was really a signet ring or seal used to sign documents and letters (Gen. 38:18). These signet rings were worn on the right hand or suspended on a chain or cord about the neck. They served as the personal signature of the owner. When this signet ring was stamped into a wet clay tablet or soft sealing wax, it left a design or imprint which represented the owner's signature.

Kings gave validity to their laws by using these signet rings, also called scarabs. They would have such a ring for each one of their responsible officials. Pharaoh gave Joseph such a ring. (Gen. 41:42). Many of these rings were set with a swivel on a band of gold. This made them more pliable for stamping the signature. Other

than the ring and the staff, men wore very little ornamentation.

Among the women this was not true. Abraham's
servant had two bracelets to give Rebekah (Gen. 24:22).
Earrings were worn by the women of Jacob's family
(Gen. 35:4). The earrings of the Israelite women were
melted in the wilderness to make the golden calf (Exod.
32:2). Isaiah lists many of the ornaments worn by the
women:

> In that day the Lord will take away the finery of the
> anklets, the headbands, and the crescents; the pendants, the
> bracelets, and the scarfs; the headdresses, the armlets, the
> sashes, the perfume boxes, and the amulets; the signet rings
> and nose rings; the festal robes, the mantles, the cloaks, and
> the handbags; the garments of gauze, the linen garments, the
> turbans, and the veils (Isa. 3:18-23).

The anklets were fastened to the ankle band of each
leg. They were admired for the jingle and tinkle they
made when walking. They were as common as bracelets (Isa. 3:16). The crescents and pendants were worn
on the ear or about the neck. They were made of colored
glass, brass, silver, and gold. The amulets were ornaments, gems, or scrolls worn on the ear or around the
neck. Sometimes they were used to ward off evil spirits
and charms. The armlet was a bracelet worn on the
upper part of the arm. Rings were worn as frequently in
the nose as on the finger.

Cosmetics

An eye paint, consisting of a paste made from colored
powder, was used by women to give brilliancy to the
eyes. Applied to the eyes of children, it was supposed to
strengthen them. Ezekiel and Jeremiah speak of women
who painted their eyes (Ezek. 23:40). Jezebel used such

cosmetics (II Kings 9:30). This paint was kept in small
ornamented jars having a brush attached to the stopper
to apply the paint to the face and eyelashes.

Face powder was stored in scallop shells from the Persian Gulf. Clay, bronze, and copper boxes were used to
store the cosmetics. The toilet kit contained the paint
stick, tweezers, combs, and powder boxes. Perfume was
in common usage among the Hebrew women. Some
women were fortunate enough to have polished bronze
mirrors.

CHAPTER FOUR

Customs at Home

It is one of the oddities of history that the people of the Orient did not change appreciably in their mode of living from the days of Abraham through New Testament times. The climate, natural resources, and the culture were such that change was resisted even more than is normally true. Customs and manners were handed down from one generation to the next and were carefully guarded.

Hospitality

Throughout all this time a distinguishing characteristic of the people of Bible lands was hospitality. For them it was a sacred duty. They believed that a guest in their home was sent to them by God. Perfect strangers were welcomed into the home as if they were friends or neighbors. The Orientals have a proverb which says, "Every stranger is an invited guest." The arrival of strangers was a rare and welcome occasion.

When Abraham, sitting in his tent door, saw three strangers coming toward him, he ran to meet them and welcomed them into his home and fellowship. He asked Sarah, his wife, to make cakes while he prepared the fatted calf and set milk and butter before the company (Gen. 18:2-8).

41

The guest in the tent dweller's home shared sleeping quarters with the men. Since the people slept in their clothing, there was little need for privacy. In the small house where there was only one room, the guest ate, was entertained, and slept in this one room with the family. In larger dwellings a special guest room was provided. This might be the upper room.

When a guest came into a home, the host bowed to the ground in welcome, sometimes even falling to his knees. Then he greeted each guest with a kiss. This he did by placing his right hand on the friend's left shoulder and kissing his right cheek. Then the action was reversed; placing his left hand on the right shoulder he kissed the left cheek. A kiss was a common form of greeting between men. Jacob kissed his father (Gen. 27:27). Esau kissed Jacob (Gen. 33:4). Aaron kissed Moses (Exod. 4:27).

This type of greeting was still in vogue in New Testament times. Hence Jesus said to Simon the Pharisee, "You gave me no kiss" (Luke 7:45). Judas betrayed his Master with the sincerest kind of greeting in the Orient.

After the greeting the guest would take off his sandals. Then the host would bring a basin of water to wash the feet of the guest. The wearing of sandals in this dusty, rocky country required this practice to keep the dust of the road out of the home. In addition it was necessary because the Oriental sat on a mat or divan with his feet crossed beneath him. Abraham washed the feet of his guests (Gen. 18:4). The disciples refused to do this lowly task so Jesus girded himself with a towel and washed their feet (John 13:5).

The next duty of the host was to offer oil to anoint the head of his guest. This was a common practice with the Hebrew people. It was a mark of respect paid by a host to his guests. To abstain from this rite was a sign of mourning (Dan. 10:2-3), or lack of proper respect. The oil was poured on the head from a flask or a horn.

Olive oil was used in most cases, but sometimes it was mixed with spices. This oil would be a comfort to travelers coming into a home from the heat of a Palestinian sun. David spoke of how refreshing it was when he said, "Thou anointest my head with oil" (Psalm 23:5). This custom too was carried over into New Testament times. Simon the Pharisee neglected to do this for Jesus when He came into his Galilean home. This was a sign that Jesus was not truly welcomed as a guest (Luke 7:46).

In the early days of the Christian era it was important for the members to practice such hospitality. When the persecution began, people had to flee for their lives. It certainly was a comfort for them to know that hospitality was an unwritten law. Any Christian home was a place of refuge for one who had to flee because of his testimony for Christ.

Paul stayed in the house of Priscilla and Aquila while he carried on the work in Corinth (Acts 18:1-3). He wrote that one of the qualifications of a bishop was that he must be hospitable (I Tim. 3:2). He stressed to laymen that they, too, must "practice hospitality" (Rom. 12:13). Peter, in his letter, told the Christians to "practice hospitality ungrudgingly to one another" (I Peter 4:9). John, in his third epistle, says, "It is a loyal thing you do when you render any service to the brethren, especially to strangers . . . you will do well to send them on their journey as befits God's service" (III John 5-6). The ancient practice of hospitality fostered Christian fellowship and strengthened the faith of the persecuted.

The Patriarchal System

In the patriarchal system the father was the head of the household. The family was a little kingdom within itself. The father had supreme authority over the family, even to the right of the life and death of his children,

the children's children, and the servants. He also had
the moral obligation to protect them. It was his responsibility to administer justice to the members of the
family. His orders could not be disputed. The principal
duties of the children in this home were obedience and
reverence.

Every home had to have a father. If he should die, his
place was automatically taken by the oldest son, who then
became the "father" of the whole family. In some cases
the father might designate another of his sons to take
his place.

Reuben, the first born of Jacob, should have inherited
the birthright, but was dispossessed because of his un-
controlled passion and sin. Simeon and Levi also for-
feited their birthright because of their cruelty at Shechem. Thus the privileges of the birthright were solemnly
transferred to Judah. He was to be their leader, "the
lion" with full royal sway over all the nations. The
Messiah was to come through his family (Gen. 49:1-15).
Similarly, David placed the throne in Solomon's hands
(I Kings 1:33, 34).

When a man married he brought his bride home to his
father's house to live. Hence, the daughters always left
home to go to the house of the bridegroom. The bride
would be expected to help with the manual labor of the
clan. Thus the birth of a son was always a welcome event.
He was another defender of the family honor and would
continue the father's name. To have no son was an occasion for divorce. The birth of a daughter was often
considered a cause for sympathy or an occasion for sorrow.

In the patriarchal home the wife was in a subordinate
position. Women were never treated as equals, nor were
they ever permitted to eat with the men. The husband
and brothers were always served first; the wife and
sisters learned to wait and partake of what was left. On

a journey, the man always walked a few steps ahead of the wife, who kept at a respectful distance. As a rule women were kept closely confined within the home and watched over with jealousy.

They were not slaves, however, and in some cases they did exert a powerful influence over the husbands. Bathsheba (I Kings 2:19), Athaliah (II Kings 11:1-3), and Jezebel (I Kings 21:7-14) were women who rose to power even in politics. However, this was the exception.

The Birth of a Child

SWADDLING
CLOTHS

When a child was born it was sprinkled with salt, but was seldom washed (Ezek. 16: 4). The arms were laid at its side and it was snugly wrapped in bandages of linen or cotton, four or five inches in width and from five to six yards long. A band was also placed under the chin and over the forehead. In this way the child could hardly move a muscle of the hand or foot. These were the swaddling cloths in which Jesus was wrapped. It was believed that this wrapping would make the child healthy and strong. It also made it easy for the mother to carry him. As the child became older he was removed from these swaddling cloths.

Naming a Child

For a child's name, the parents tried to find an expression indicating something connected with birth, gratitude, hope, or inspiration. All Hebrew names had a meaning. Moses meant "drawn from water," Samuel meant "asked of God," and Cephas meant "rock."

It was also a common custom to include a name for God as a part of the child's name. A few examples of such names are: Obadiah (Servant of Jehovah); Daniel (God is my judge), Elijah (My God is Jehovah), Ezekiel (God will strengthen).

Jewish girls were often named after something beautiful or virtuous. Rachel meant "lamb," Salome meant "peace," and Dorcas meant "gazelle." Naomi told the women of Bethlehem, "Do not call me Naomi, call me Mara," for Mara meant "bitter" (Ruth 1:20-21).

Often the son added the name of his father after his own in order to indicate the family from which he came. Thus Jesus spoke of Peter as Simon Bar-Jona, or "son of Jona." The word "bar" indicates "son of." The magician in Paphos was a Jewish false prophet named Bar-Jesus, that is, "son of Jesus" (Acts 13:6).

Circumcision

Circumcision was a rite practiced by the Israelites since the days of Abraham. God selected Abraham to be the father of his chosen people. They were to become as numerous as the sands of the sea and the stars of the heaven (Gen. 22:17). From this chosen family, the long-awaited Messiah was to come. As a token of this covenant of God with His people, circumcision was made mandatory. To fail to comply with this command of God meant that the person would be cut off forever from the Israelite family.

Moses established this rite as a national ordinance among the Jews, and Joshua continued the practice after the people entered the promised land. Only the male members of the family were subjected to this operation.

It was to be performed on the eighth day after the birth
of a son (Lev. 12:13). It seems to have been the custom
to give the child his name on the day he was circum-
cised (Luke 1:59). Male slaves that were taken into the
Israelite family were also forced to submit to this regula-
tion. No one could become a proselyte to the Jewish
religion without this rite. No uncircumcised male could
enter the temple or partake of the Passover Feast. The
Sacrament of Baptism replaced this Old Testament rite
in the Christian era.

Selection of a Life Mate

Parents selected a bride for their son. The new bride
became a member of the family clan; therefore the whole
family was interested in knowing if she would be suit-
able. Sometimes the parents consulted the bride to see
if she were willing to go into this new clan. Rebekah
was asked if she would be willing to go and become the
wife of Isaac (Gen. 24:58). But the parents felt that they
had the right to make the final choice.

Marriage demanded a dowry from the groom to the
bride's father. Wives were regarded by law as property.
When a daughter was given in marriage, her family was
actually diminishing its efficiency. Unmarried daughters
took care of the flocks, worked in the fields, or helped in
other ways. Thus when a young woman married she
would increase the efficiency of her husband's clan.
Therefore, the young man who expected to get posses-
sion of a daughter must compensate with a dowry, which
was a gift of flocks or herds.

Sometimes a part of the dowry would be given to the
bride as a gift. The father often gave gifts to the bride
when she left home. Rebekah's father gave her a nurse
and maids when she went to Isaac (Gen. 24:59-61). Caleb

gave his daughter a gift of a field with springs of water
(Judg. 1:15).

Betrothal

The betrothal was really a covenant of marriage. The
families of the bride and groom met with some wit-
nesses not included in the family group. The young man
gave the bride a ring of gold, or some article of value;
in some cases it was only a document in which he promised to marry the girl. Then he would say, "See by this
ring (or token) thou art set aside for me according to the
law of Moses and of Israel." This betrothal was as binding as marriage. At least a whole year passed between
the betrothal and the actual marriage.

The Wedding

The real marriage consisted simply in the groom coming to take the bride to the family home to live. Not until
this date did the couple actually live together. The groom
wore his very best for this great occasion. He dressed as
much like a king as possible. Isaiah was thinking of this
preparation of the groom when he said, "He has covered
me with the robe of righteousness, as a bridegroom decks
himself with a garland" (Isa. 61:10). Dressed in all of
his finery, the groom went with his friends to the house
of the bride to bring her to his home.

The adornment of the bride was also a costly affair.
Everything possible was done to prepare her to receive
her husband. Her hair was braided and interwoven with
jewels, if the family could afford it. Often jewels were
borrowed from friends for this occasion. Little wonder
that John spoke of the New Jerusalem as a "bride
adorned for her husband" (Rev. 21:2). The bride left
her father's house in all of her finery and perfume, with

a crown on her head. Ezekiel gave a good description of this: "I decked you with ornaments, and put bracelets on your arms, and a chain on your neck. And I put a ring on your nose, and earrings in your ears, and a beautiful crown upon your head" (Ezek. 16:11-12).

There was no religious ceremony in the wedding. The groom simply brought the bride to his father's house. This was a signal for feasting which continued for an entire week. Friends, neighbors, and relatives stayed in the home during all this time.

The bride in the home of her husband's father was now legally a piece of clan property. She was assigned a share of the duties of the household.

Divorce

The stability of the family was founded on the absolute authority of the father. He could divorce his wife without giving any explanation and without assuming any obligation for her support. Just a spoken word to that effect was required for the divorce. The Israelite woman could not divorce her husband, because he owned her; but she could be sent away from the home at a moment's notice. If there was no son, if she burned the food, or if the husband found a more desirable wife, he might ask for a divorce. The wife could take with her the clothes that she was wearing. For this reason the coins on her headgear, rings, bracelets, armlets, anklets, and necklaces were very important. She was always in danger of becoming a substitute to a second wife whom her husband might acquire and prefer.

Moses demanded, however, that the husband must give his divorced wife a written bill of divorcement (Deut. 24:1). Jesus pushed aside other reasons and made unfaithfulness the only grounds for divorce (Matt. 5: 31-32).

Death in the Home

Death always was a deep tragedy to these people.
Those watching by the bedside raised a shrieking wail
as soon as life departed. This was a signal for loud
mourning. Friends and relatives crowded into the house
and practiced all of the customary signs of grief. They
tore their hair, beat their breasts, and cried out loudly
until sheer physical exhaustion brought on dullness and

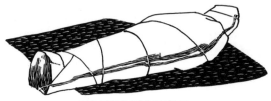

WRAPPED FOR BURIAL

depression. As each new group of friends came into the
home, the wailing rose in volume.

The mourners often tried to speak to the departed
one or to other members of the family who were
dead in order to force themselves to cry out afresh. When
an unmarried person died, the event was made all the
more pathetic by first going through some form of a
wedding ceremony. Hired mourners were often employed.

Elisha rent his clothes when Elijah was taken into
heaven (II Kings 2:12). In other words he ripped the
robe he was wearing as a sign of sheer anguish. Amos
spoke of putting sackcloth on the body (Amos 8:10).
This was a coarse, rough material signifying that death
brought a loss of desire for the finery of life.

The art of embalming had not come into practice in
Palestine, so the burial occurred on the day of death
if at all possible. The body was generally dressed in a

single cloak, or wrapped in a sheet. It was then placed
on a bier and carried out to the place of burial. Friends
vied with each other for the privilege of acting as bear-
ers. Only men accompanied the body to its resting place.
The women could go later if they so desired.

Tombs were usually cut out of rock in a family garden.
Joseph of Arimathea asked that the body of Jesus might
rest in his garden tomb (Matt. 27:59-60). Large, round,
wheel-like stones were rolled into place in a groove in
front of the tomb to give privacy to the burial place.
These stones were not boulders, as artists are prone to
paint. Some constructed elaborate tombs. The poor,
however, often used caves.

CHAPTER FIVE

STONE ALTAR

Alms and Altars

People of the Orient have always been deeply religious. To be without religion was to live in a moral void. To deny the existence of God was considered impossible —to prove it, unnecessary. Skepticism was considered the self defense of a disobedient heart.

Accordingly, the life of the Jewish people was religious from the cradle to the grave. Their religion was a part of their daily life. Religious activities at first centered in the home, in both Old and New Testaments. Parents had a solemn duty to bring up their children in the fear of the Lord. The Law of Moses was specific at this point.

The father was the priest of the household. It was his responsibility to train the children to "love the Lord their God." He taught them the Law of Moses and explained the meaning of religious observances. He told them about the Covenant with God and the implications of that relationship. Parents were commanded to review the providential acts of God throughout their history in Egypt and Canaan. "Make them known to your children and your children's children" (Deut. 4:9), was God's instruction. It was from their father that children heard the promise of a Messiah and of salvation in His name.

If the father died, this responsibility was passed on to the oldest son.

Son of the Law

At 13 years of age the Jewish boy became what was known as a "son of the law," "son of the commandment," or "son of the Torah." The boy was now obliged to learn the law and observe all of its provisions. The Pentateuch became his textbook. He was now regarded as an adult and as such was pledged to the entire law.

Now the boy had to be careful not to touch anything that was unclean, such as Gentiles, hogs, or a dead body. He must walk only so far on the Sabbath day. When he went to the synagogue he must now wear the prescribed dress for men and join in the prayers. He was made personally responsible in all religious matters. The young boy was always proud to do these things as it made him feel that now at last he was a man.

It was in accordance with this custom that Jesus made the long journey to Jerusalem after He had reached His twelfth birthday. To assume these responsibilities must have been an exciting experience. Now He could take His place alongside of the rest of the men in the temple worship.

The Altar

In early times religious observances in the home centered around an altar where animals were sacrificed and offered to God. When Abraham came into Canaan he pitched his tent at Bethel and "there he built an altar to the Lord and called on the name of the Lord" (Gen. 12:8). When he came to Hebron he built another altar (Gen. 13:18). Jacob built an altar at Shechem (Gen. 33: 18-20). When God spoke to him he built an altar at Bethel, as his grandfather had done (Gen. 35:3). These early altars were simply tiers of stones piled on top of each other. They helped to produce a sense of sin, a realization of the holiness of God, and an assurance that God could be reached through a sacrifice.

Later when God gave instructions for constructing the tabernacle in the wilderness, sacrifices were made at the altar of the holy place (Exod. 26:1-37). This eliminated the private altars of each family. After the completion of Solomon's temple in Jerusalem, the sacrifices were offered by the priests at the great altar in the holy place of the temple.

Almsgiving, Prayer, and Fasting

Almsgiving, prayer, and fasting were the chief aspects of worship. Alms were given because the people felt that the poor were in their circumstances by the will of God and would always be found in the nation (Deut. 15:11). Hence he who gave to the poor was lending to the Lord, who would repay him (Prov. 19:17). Everyone was expected to give alms to the beggar on the corner of the street and at the city gate.

Prayer was communion with God. The people cried out to the Lord in times of need; thanked Him for His blessings, and asked for guidance. No directions concerning prayer were given in the Mosaic law. The duty of prayer was taken for granted. In Jerusalem it was the custom to go to the temple to pray. Those who were not in the holy city would "open their windows toward Jerusalem" and pray towards the place of God's presence (I Kings 8:46-59, Dan. 6:10).

There were three regular hours of prayer: in the morning at 9 o'clock, at noon, and at 3 o'clock in the afternoon (Psalm 55:17). Peter prayed at noon on the housetop of Simon the Tanner in Joppa (Acts 10:9). Peter and John were going to the temple to pray at the 3 o'clock hour when they met the lame man (Acts 3:1).

Table grace before eating was a common practice (Acts 27:35).

The posture of prayer among the Israelites was most often a standing position. The hands were sometimes held upward with palms uplifted in supplication. The head was usually held upward. Humiliation was expressed in kneeling (I Kings 8:54). Prostration was sometimes practiced (Neh. 8:6).

Prayer shawls were apparently used by the men in the synagogue during New Testament times.

Fasting was also a part of worship. It was observed with various degrees of strictness. Sometimes there was entire abstinence from food (Esther 4:16). On other occasions it appears to have been only a restriction to a very plain diet (Dan. 10:3).

Only one fast day a year was appointed by law. But it came to be a common religious practice. The days of fasting were observed on the second and fifth days of the week. Fasts were an indication of sorrow for sin, of gratefulness to God for His mercy, and of dependence upon God in times of grave danger. Those who fasted frequently dressed in rough, coarse sackcloth, put ashes on their forehead, and went barefoot (I Kings 21:27). Ashes and earth placed on the forehead were a sign of mourning and sorrow (II Sam. 15:32). Fasting was an indication of the sacrifice of the personal will to God.

During the Babylonian captivity the Jews observed four annual fasts, in the fourth, fifth, seventh, and tenth months (Zech. 7:1-8, 8:19). Public fasts were occasionally proclaimed by the rulers to express national humiliation or to gain the favor of God (I Sam. 7:6, Jer. 36:6-10). After the captivity, weekly fasts were instituted by the priests. They were observed on the second and fifth days of the week. These fasts were carried over into New Testament times (Mark 2:18). The Pharisees prided themselves on their observation of these fasts (Luke 18:12).

Music and Religion

RAM'S HORN

TRUMPET

Music played a very important part in the religious life of these people. Several types of instruments were used, either alone or to accompany singing. Jubal apparently was the pioneer maker of such instruments. The Bible says, "He was the father of all those who play the lyre and pipe" (Gen. 4:21).

The trumpets used were of three types. The earliest ones were made of the horn of an ox or a ram. A second type was made of metal and curved like an ox horn. A later form was straight, like trumpets of today. God commanded Moses to make two silver trumpets to call the people together (Num. 10:2). The year of Jubilee was ushered in by the blowing of trumpets (Lev. 25:8-9).

The timbrel was used for banquets and for religious gatherings. After the victory over the Egyptians at the Red Sea, Miriam, the sister of Moses, went out with a timbrel in her hand, and all of the women followed her to sing and dance (Ex. 15:20). This timbrel was a circular hoop made either of wood or brass and covered with tightly-drawn skin. Bells hung around it. It was similar to the modern tambourine.

TIMBREL

The harp was similar to the lyre, a small instrument which could be played as it was carried about. It was held upside down, with its sound box, which gave resonance to the strings, at the top. From the sound box two rods, curved or straight, extended outward and were connected by a crosspiece, to which the strings were attached. The most famous harp player was David.

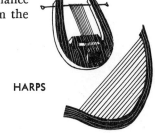

HARPS

The "organ" was really a pipe, and was more like the flute than any other instrument. When Jesus came into Jairus' home He saw the flute played (Matt. 9:23). The flute was simply a double pipe.

The psaltery and viol were stringed instruments. There is no way of knowing their exact shape. Cymbals were like present-day cymbals, brass plates of convex form which made a ringing sound when clanged together. Even the bagpipe was used (Dan. 3:5).

The Book of Psalms was really a hymnbook. Psalms were sung antiphonally by dividing the company into two bands. One group sang a phrase and the other group gave the response. All united on the final line (Ezra 3:11).

FLUTE

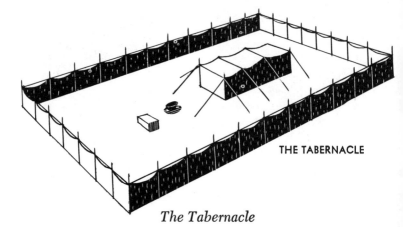

THE TABERNACLE

The Tabernacle

As indicated above, during the days of Abraham, Isaac, Jacob, and Joseph there was no appointed place of worship. Sacrifices were offered on the family altar. The first tabernacle or tent of meeting was set up by Moses and Aaron in the wilderness. This tent church was dedicated to communion with God. It was made so that it could be easily moved from one place to the other as the people wandered in the wilderness.

The court surrounding the tabernacle was an oblong space 150 feet long and 75 feet wide. It was surrounded by canvas screens, seven and one-half feet high, supported by pillars of brass, seven and one-half feet apart. The canvas was attached to the pillars with hooks and fillets of silver. The entrance of the eastern end was 30 feet wide and closed by curtains of fine twined linen embroidered with needle work of the most gorgeous colors. In the eastern half of the court stood the altar of burnt offerings and the laver where the priests washed their hands and feet.

The tabernacle itself was placed in the western end of the court. It was an oblong structure 45 feet long, 15

feet wide, and 15 feet in
height. The interior of this
tabernacle was divided into
two chambers. The first or
outer one was 30 feet long.
This room was called the
Holy Place. It contained
the golden candlestick and

LAVER

the table for the bread of the Presence (showbread) and
the altar of incense.

The second room, called the Most Holy Place, was a
cube of 15 feet. This room contained the Ark of the
Covenant, surmounted by the cherubim. The veil, a
sumptuous curtain embroidered with cherubim, divided
the Holy Place from the Most Holy Place.

The decorations and furnishings symbolized the people's religious beliefs. They were designed to show that
God was holy and righteous.

The Ark of the Covenant

In the Most Holy Place was kept the Ark of the Covenant. This was a wooden chest, lined with gold, about
four and one-half feet in length and two feet in height

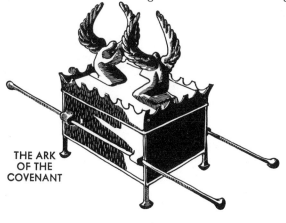

THE ARK
OF THE
COVENANT

and breadth (Ex. 25:10-22). Its cover was of pure gold. Into this ark were placed the two tablets of stone, a pot of manna (Ex. 16:31-36), and the rod of Aaron (Num. 17:1-11).

This movable tabernacle with its Ark of the Covenant was in use until the Hebrews were finally settled in the Promised Land. Then a more permanent home was made to house the Ark. The city of Shiloh became the headquarters of the priests, and a building of brick or stone became the place of worship.

The Temple
of
Solomon

When Jerusalem became the center of the nation during the reign of David, the king longed for a beautiful temple where God could be worshipped and the Ark of the Covenant set up permanently. But David himself was not permitted to build such a temple (II Sam. 7:4-16). This task was left to his son Solomon.

Solomon had magnificent ideas about construction and adornment. Hiram, the king of Tyre, furnished cedar for the temple and agreed to loan skilled workmen to Solomon. Thus all of the artistry and skill of Phoenicia went into this temple.

It was oblong in shape, about 124 feet long and 55 feet wide. The front of the temple faced east. Here a great folding door opened onto a porch. On either side of this door stood a large bronze pillar (I Kings 7:15).

The temple was divided into two rooms, the **Holy Place** and the Most Holy Place, the latter being the smaller of the two. A heavy curtain separated these rooms. Only the high priest was permitted to go into the Most Holy Place, and he could enter only once a year to sprinkle blood on the mercy seat (the cover of the Ark).

Two great figures of cherubim, carved from olive wood and overlaid with gold, were placed on either side of the Ark. These figures were 15 feet in height. The length of the wings from tip to tip was 15 feet. The wings were so great that they touched each other and the outer wings touched the walls. "The wings of the cherubim were spread out so that a wing of one touched the one wall, and a wing of the other cherub touched the other wall; their other wings touched each other in the middle of the house" (I Kings 6:27).

In the courts around the temple stood the altars, lavers, and water tanks used in the sacrifices. These outer courts were no doubt double the size of the tabernacle. They probably extended 150 feet from north to south, and 300 feet from east to west. The temple area enclosed by the outer walls formed a square of about 600 feet.

It took seven and one-half years to build this temple. It stood for 350 years, until Nebuchadnezzar destroyed it in the year 586 B.C. At that time most of the Hebrews were carried to Babylon as prisoners, together with the temple treasures of gold and silver.

The Temple of Zerubbabel

For nearly 70 years the lovely temple of Solomon lay in ruins. In the meantime Babylon fell to the Persians. Then Cyrus, the great Persian king, gave permission for the Jews to return to Jerusalem to rebuild the city, its walls, and the temple. This movement back to Jerusalem was led by Zerubbabel (Ezra 4:1-2).

The temple built at this time was apparently constructed on the same pattern as Solomon's. However, the magnificence of the first temple was never achieved. The

FLOOR PLAN

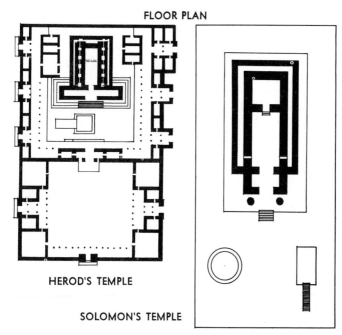

HEROD'S TEMPLE

SOLOMON'S TEMPLE

returning exiles were too poor. They could not hire the skilled workmen that Solomon had. The sacred Ark was gone. It probably was burned by Nebuchadnezzar or taken away because of its gold. When the old men who had seen the glory of Solomon's temple saw the new one they wept because of its inferiority (Ezra 3:12). The second temple stood for five centuries. The Greeks robbed and defiled it. The Romans plundered it mercilessly when they captured the city.

The Temple of Herod

When Herod was appointed governor of Judea he promised the people that he would build for them a new temple. The work started about 20 B.C., which was about sixteen years before the birth of Jesus. The actual construction of the main buildings required about eight years. The courts were not really completed until around 62-64 A.D., just a few years before the entire structure was destroyed. Little wonder that the people doubted the validity of Jesus' statement, "Destroy this temple, and in three days I will raise it up" (John 2:19).

This time Roman architecture was used. No doubt Herod used many of the stones of the first two temples. However, he covered his temple with white marble and gilt. It was larger than the temple of Solomon. The inner enclosure was about 270 feet wide and 360 feet long, and was adorned with porches and magnificent gateways. It was on Solomon's Porch that Peter preached to the people after the healing of the lame man (Acts 3:11). An outer enclosure measuring 600 feet each way, with porticos of great splendor, stretched beyond the inner area. So this temple occupied an area four or five times greater than the two temples that preceded it.

The temple proper was 120 feet long, 60 feet wide, and 45 feet high. This was divided into three parts. The porch was 15 feet deep and extended all across the temple. The front of the porch was supported by two gigantic bronze pillars 27 feet high, topped with capitals seven feet high. The Holy Place was 60 feet long and 30 feet wide. The Most Holy Place was a 30-foot cube. In this inner room was placed the Ark and the cherubim.

Between the two rooms was hung a curtain. It was made of fine linen, embroidered in blue, scarlet, and purple. Cherubim were skillfully worked into its design. It was hung on four pillars of wood overlaid with gold. The veil was fastened with clasps to these pillars. This was the veil torn asunder at the death of Jesus (Matt. 27:51).

The temple had nine gates. The eastern gate, opposite Solomon's Porch, was made from Corinthian brass and was called the "Gate Beautiful" (Acts 3:2). This was the most famous of the gates. Higher than the other gates, it was made in the form of a vine. The entire gate was adorned with silver and gold. It was made in Greece and purchased by Herod. Six men were required to open and close it. When the morning sun shone upon it, it glistened like a wall of gold.

The inner courts included courts for the women, the men, Gentile proselytes, and the priests.

The "outer court" was the same as the "court of the Gentiles." The surface of this court was paved with colored stones. A stone wall separated it from the "inner court" or "court of the Israelites." This wall was about 50 inches high. On the columns of this wall were hung signs written in Greek and Latin that no heathen or Gentile, under penalty of death, could go beyond this partition.

Herod built this outer court so that his Gentile subjects, who were Egyptians, Greeks, or Romans, could be allowed to go into a part of the temple. This large outer court was open to all nationalities who wished to enter some part of the sanctuary. Here buying, selling, and the exchange of money were permitted. This was where Jesus came to cleanse the temple.

The colonnades around the sides of the outer court provided open places where people would gather for discussions. Here the doctors of law and other learned men met to interpret the law. This was probably the place where Jesus was discoursing with the teachers when His parents left for Nazareth.

This lovely temple was destroyed in 70 A.D. under the siege of the Romans. Since that date there has never been a temple to the Jewish faith in Jerusalem.

THE SYNAGOGUE

The Synagogue

During the Babylonian exile of 70 years, the Jews felt the need of coming together to talk over the things of God, and to pray for their deliverance and restoration to the homeland. The Sabbath day was the logical time for this. At first homes were probably used for meeting places. Later, special buildings were erected for this purpose. These were called synagogues. When Jews traveled from place to place they naturally looked for people of their own nationality. The synagogue became the logical place to find this fellowship. On his missionary journeys, Paul always sought out the local synagogue.

In the synagogue the men with the most learning helped those with little or none. Not all read the scrolls, but all took part in the chanting of the psalms. The synagogues became the centers of learning. Little boys went there every day to learn to read Hebrew and the scrolls. Services, which included prayer, praise, reading of the scrolls, and instruction, were held every Sabbath day. If a distinguished visitor came to the synagogue he was invited to speak. So it was that when Jesus preached in the synagogue of Nazareth, His own people rejected Him (Luke 4:16-30). Because of this practice Paul was able to give his Christian witness in many cities (Acts 13:14-15).

The Early Christian Churches

The earliest gathering places for the Christians were in homes. The church in Jerusalem met in the home of Mary, the mother of Mark (Acts 12:12). Priscilla and Aquila opened their home for a congregation (I Cor. 16:19). Paul asked Philemon to greet the "church in your house" (Philemon 2). Joseph P. Free, in his book, *Archaeology and Bible History,* says,

The earliest church which has yet been excavated and dated with certainty comes from the third century A.D. at Dura in Mesopotamia, on the Euphrates River. This was merely a room in a house which had been set apart and furnished as a chapel for worship.*

---

*Joseph P. Free, *Archaeology and the Bible* (Van Kampen Press, Wheaton, Ill., 1950) , p. 335.

CHAPTER SIX

Holy Days

As religious observances began to be focused at a central sanctuary for the entire nation, a number of ceremonies and special holy days came to be observed, each with its customs and regulations. An important part of the religious life of the Hebrews was a pilgrimage to the place of the sanctuary or temple. "Three times in the year shall all your males appear before the Lord God, the God of Israel" (Ex. 34:23).

The whole family could go if they desired, but men were required to make these pilgrimages.

Elkanah was accustomed to take his wife and make this journey. "Now this man used to go up year by year from his city to worship and to sacrifice to the Lord of hosts at Shiloh" (I Sam. 1:3). It was on one of these pilgrimages that Hannah prayed for a son, and in due time the baby Samuel was born.

The most famous journey to the feasts, of course, was the one made by Joseph, Mary, and the 12-year-old boy Jesus. "Now his parents went to Jerusalem every year at the feast of the Passover. And when he was 12 years old, they went up according to custom" (Luke 2:41-42). How Jesus must have been filled with anticipation as they set out on the journey to the holy city! Every Jewish boy had to make this journey to Jerusalem after his twelfth birthday to be made a "son of the Covenant."

The Feast of the Passover

The first of these feasts was the Passover. It was also referred to as the Feast of Unleavened Bread. The first celebration of the Passover was held in Egypt when God's chosen people were to be brought out of that foreign land of bondage. The word of the Lord came to Moses with minute instructions for preparing and eating the feast.

On the tenth day of the month Abid, the head of each family was to select a male lamb without blemish and one year old. On the fourteenth day of the month the lamb was to be killed when the sun was setting. The blood was to be caught in a basin and sprinkled on the doorposts and the lintel.

The lamb was then roasted whole. It could not be boiled, nor could a bone of it be broken. Unleavened bread and bitter herbs were to be eaten with the lamb. Everyone was to have his staff ready, his shoes on his feet, and his loins girded—ready to travel immediately. They were to eat in haste. At midnight there was weeping and lamentation in the Egyptian homes when they discovered that the oldest son in every family was dead. Pharaoh and his people urged the Israelites to leave immediately. In haste they left that very day (Ex. 12:1-51).

The father explained to the family the purpose of God in smiting the first-born of every Egyptian family. The father told them that from now on this Passover was to be a national ordinance. They were to teach their children and children's children the meaning of the feast.

In later times the annual celebration of this feast varied from its first institution, as circumstances were

much different after the Hebrews became a settled people. The Passover was held from the fourteenth to the
end of the twenty-first of the Jewish month Nisan, which
corresponds to April (Ex. 12:6, 18). This was a season
of great rejoicing, preceded by feverish preparation in
the Jewish families. It was the beginning of the Jewish
religious year. When the sun set on the fourteenth day,
and the stars began to appear, everything had to be in
readiness for the celebration. The house had been
cleaned and all the food prepared. Members of the
family were dressed in their newest clothes.

The celebration began with the reading of the Scriptures in the Hebrew tongue. The head of the family
explained the purpose of the feast and the circumstance
under which the Passover was instituted. The father
would then ask each of the sons present where they were
going and he would receive from each one the same
answer, "I am going from the land of Egypt to the land
of Jerusalem." Four cups of wine diluted with water
were set aside to be drunk during the celebration. It had
to be wine of the best quality and free from contamination by Gentiles.

During the preparation for this feast great care was
taken to rid the house of leaven and leavened bread
since leaven was an indication of fermentation and
thereby contamination. Every utensil for making, hold-
ing, or storing leavened bread had to be removed. In
making the unleavened bread, great care was observed
that no crumb of leavened bread should fall into the
dough. This bread could be made of wheat, spelt, barley,
oats, or rye, but not of rice or millet. It was probably
formed into dry, thin biscuits. The unleavened bread
was eaten in commemoration of the hasty flight into
Egypt; haste that would not allow for the ordinary
leavened dough to rise. It also indicated the poverty and
suffering under Pharaoh.

The Passover lamb was roasted whole. The law for-
mally allowed the alternative of a kid, but a lamb was
always preferred (Ex. 12:5). The lamb was slain at the
temple. The fat and blood were given to the priests (II
Chron. 35:11-14). The fat was burned and the blood
was sprinkled on the altar. The lamb was then roasted.
Any uneaten flesh had to be burned the morning after
the feast. No part of the lamb was to be carried out of
the house.

The people also ate bitter herbs in commemoration of
the bitter suffering they had experienced at the hands
of the Egyptians. These bitter herbs could be endive,
chicory, or wild lettuce. The feast was celebrated in
family groups of not less than ten people nor more than
20. No male who was uncircumcised could partake of the
Passover. The celebration of this feast lasted for eight
days.

The Feast of Pentecost

The second great feast of the Hebrews was Pentecost.
This must not be confused with the Pentecost of the
New Testament. The Holy Spirit came upon the disciples on the day of the celebration of the Old Testament
feast, hence the term Pentecost was carried over into the
Christian Church. The Old Testament Pentecost occurred 50 days after the beginning of the Passover, on
the seventh day of the Jewish month Sivan which is
about the same as our month of June. It was also called
the Feast of Harvest (Ex. 23:16), or the Feast of Weeks
(Deut. 16:9-12).

This feast lasted only one day. In the temple, offerings
were made of bread from the new crop of wheat. This
bread could contain leaven. Two loaves of this bread
were brought to the priest for the wave offering before
the altar of the Lord. This rite was a part of the peace
offering. The two loaves of bread were to be "waved"

and then offered with two lambs. It was to be a "waving" before Jehovah.

In addition, a kid was sacrificed as a sin offering, and a burnt offering of a young bullock, two rams, and seven lambs was given. There was also a drink offering in connection with this festival.

Until this feast was celebrated, the produce of the harvest could not be eaten. It was a dedication of their crops to God.

The Feast of Tabernacles

The third great festival of the Jewish people was the Feast of Tabernacles. This feast began after sunset on the fourteenth of the Jewish month Tishri, which is comparable to our October. It was their Thanksgiving Day for the ingathering of the fruits of the summer, especially grain, raisins, figs, and olives. The feast lasted for seven days, yet they always observed the eighth day as a day of holy convocation.

During this feast the Jews erected tabernacles or booths, made out of the branches of palm trees or reeds, upon the rooftops of their homes or in the courtyard. This commemorated the days when they dwelt in tents in the wilderness. For a whole week they lived out-of-doors in these booths, or tent houses. It is from these booths that the feast received its name. Boughs were plaited together to make the sides and the roof. The front was usually left open to the weather. They tried to make these little booths as beautiful as possible.

This was the most joyous of the feasts (Deut. 16:13-16). All cares were laid aside for this time of celebrating the generosity of God. People came from all over the land. As they entered the city they marched to the temple in procession, carrying baskets of grain and fruit, singing verses from the Psalms as they wound their way to the temple. All the gifts were placed by the side of the altar as they worshipped God silently. There was much singing and the music of harps, cymbals, and trumpets, for it was a joyous thanksgiving time for mercies past and present.

The Feast of Purim

A lesser feast, yet one which meant a great deal to the Jews, was the Feast of Purim. This commemorated the frustration of the plot to massacre the Jews through the wisdom of Queen Esther and Mordecai, her uncle, during the captivity in Babylon (Esther 9:26-28). This feast did not have to be celebrated in the temple at Jerusalem as the other feasts did. The story of Esther was always read in the synagogue during the Feast of Purim. The festival lasted for two days, and was regularly observed on the fourteenth and fifteenth of the month Adar, which is our September.

The Feast of Lights

The Feast of Lights was celebrated in commemoration of the glad time when Judas Maccabaeus drove the enemy out of the temple. The Greeks had conquered Palestine and had set up idols in the temple and defiled its holy place. The Jews rallied under Maccabaeus, drove out the enemy, and cleansed the temple. The temple was rededicated and a great service of praise and thanksgiving was held.

This event took place between the two Testaments, hence its story is not recorded in Scripture. The feast was instituted on the twenty-fifth day of the ninth month, called Chisleu, in 170 B.C. During this feast the temple was ablaze with lights as the worshippers carried palm leaves in procession. Fathers related the stories of Judas

Maccabaeus to their sons. This feast could also be celebrated in the synagogues. Regulations for its observance
are recorded in the two apocryphal books, I and II Maccabees.

The Feast of the New Moon

The first day of the lunar month was observed as a
holy day. Two young bullocks, a ram, and seven one-
year-old lambs were offered as sacrifices. Flour, oil, and
wine were mixed with these offerings, and a kid was
sacrificed for a sin offering. All work ceased and a public
worship was held in the temple (Ezek. 46:3). The
trumpets were sounded to announce the offering of the
special sacrifices for the day. Great banquets were held
(I Sam. 20:5-29).

On the thirtieth day of the month the watchmen stood
on the heights around Jerusalem to observe the sky. As
soon as each of them detected the moon, he hastened to
a designated place in the city where he was examined
by the president of the Sanhedrin. When it was assured
that this was the new moon, the president rose up and
said, "It is consecrated." Immediately this information
was sent throughout all the land by torches from the tops
of the hills.

The seventh new moon of the religious year, coming
in the month of Tishri, was observed in a special way.
It was considered a day of holy convocation (Lev. 23:
24-25, Num. 29:1-6).

The Day of Atonement

The Day of Atonement was a very special day for the
Hebrews. It fell on the tenth of Tishri (our September
or October). This day was permanently instituted by
Moses, through the command of God (Lev. 16:1-34), as

a special day of atonement for sin. It was a day of
fasting; the only fast day commanded by Moses. The
day began at sunset, on the ninth of Tishri, and continued for 24 hours, or until three stars could be dis-
cerned in the sky.

The high priest spent seven days in preparation for
this day. During this time he remained in nearly solitary
confinement and abstained from all that was unclean.
He was to wear a linen coat and linen breeches, and be
girded with a linen girdle. His turban was to be of
linen. Before dressing, he was carefully bathed.

When everything was in readiness, the high priest
could step in behind the heavy curtain that separated
the Holy Place from the Most Holy Place. On no other
day was the high priest or any other priest permitted in
this part of the tabernacle or temple.

Four entries were made by the high priest into this
awesome place on the Day of Atonement. The first
entrance was to bring in the censer and the vessel of incense which were to remain in the Most Holy Place
during the entire service. When this task was accom-
plished, the high priest was to back out into the Holy
Place again so as not to turn his back to the mercy seat.

On his second entrance he took with him the blood of
the bullock, which he offered for the expiation of his
own personal sins and for those of the other priests. His
third entrance was to sprinkle blood on the mercy seat for
the sins of the people of Israel. His last entrance into
the Most Holy Place was to remove the censer and the
vessel of incense. The remainder of the day was spent
in prayer and other works of penance.

An interesting part of the service was the selecting of
two goats, identical in color, size, and age. One goat was
killed and its blood used in the service. A special ceremony was conducted over the other goat. The high
priest placed his hand upon the head of this goat and

confessed the sins of Israel over the animal. Then the goat was sent away into the wilderness. The goat was to bear the iniquities of the people into a solitary land.

The Lord made a special promise to those going to the temple for the celebration of the great feasts: "Neither shall any man desire your land, when you go up to appear before the Lord" (Exod. 34:24). God promised to protect the homes from possible enemy attack while the men were attending the festivals of the church.

The Sabbath

The Sabbath began on Friday evening at sundown. Friday was called the day of preparation. No business transactions were started unless they could be completed by sunset that evening. On Friday all of the food for the day of rest was made ready. The Sabbath was never a fast day, so much food was prepared. Elaborate means were devised to keep the food warm, as no fire could be built (Exod. 35:3). As soon as the sun set, the oil lamp was lighted, family prayers were prayed, and stories from the Old Testament were related to the children.

On the Sabbath morning the entire family went to the synagogue service. The synagogue was the most imposing building in the community. No structure was permitted to "look down" on the synagogue. The father washed his hands in the court in preparation for the service, and then entered the center door with the rest of the men of the congregation.

The women and the boys under 12 years of age had to go around to the side where they found some stone steps which led up to a second story. Here they entered a gallery that ran around three sides of the building. In front of the gallery was a wooden grill so the women and boys could see and hear the reader, while they themselves would be barely discernible. This was the women's gallery.

In the middle of the synagogue floor was a structure about twice the height of a man. It was called "ark." On top of this ark were the Scrolls, or their copy of the Old Testament. When the service began, the ruler of the Synagogue climbed the ladder-like stairs and took his seat near the Scrolls. He was not a teacher but was held in high honor in the community. It was his duty to keep the sacred Scrolls in good condition. He appointed the reader and the speaker for the day.

If there were not ten men present, they could not hold a service. If there were more than ten men the service began by the appointment of the reader. The reader stepped up to the desk to lead the congregation in the reciting of the "Shema" which was their confession of faith or creed:

Hear, O Israel: The Lord our God is one Lord; and you shall love the Lord your God with all your heart, and with all your soul, and with all your might. And these words which I command you this day shall be upon your heart; and you shall teach them diligently to your children, and shall talk of them when you sit in your house, and when you walk by the way, and when you lie down, and when you rise. And you shall bind them as a sign upon your hand, and they shall be as frontlets between your eyes. And you shall write them on the doorposts of your house and on your gates (Deut. 6:4-9).

The men chanted these words in unison.

When this was completed the ruler took the Scroll of the Law from its place in the ark and gave it to the reader. The Scroll was usually made of the skin of a goat, dried and scraped until it was as thin as a sheet of paper. On this the Old Testament was written by hand. This long narrow sheet of parchment was fastened to spindles, one on each end. The reader had to unroll or roll the Scroll until he found the passage that he wanted to read. When he finished reading, he rolled up the Scroll and gave it back to the ruler of the synagogue.

After the law was read the speaker gave the sermon or explanation of the Law. This was usually based on the Tradition of the Elders, a set of interpretations or commentaries on passages of the Law, handed down from past generations of scholars. These often went into great detail on what was or was not allowable according to the law.

One of the traditions was that of Corban (Mark 7:9-13). Corban was money set aside for the Lord and the temple. Jewish law required that aging parents were to be provided for by their family. When the children did not want to assume this responsibility they would pronounce "corban" over their world's goods. This meant that their money was set aside for the Lord and could not be used to support their parents. In this way they did not need to provide for their aged parents and could thus set aside the law of God.

Another tradition stated that when observing the religious ceremony of purification a person should hold his hands in the air as they were washed so that the soiled water would run off from his elbows. This gave assurance that no polluted water was left on the fingers. They were also concerned about who poured the water and the kind of water used in this ceremony. Unclean hands would pollute the food they ate, which in turn would make their bodies unclean.

Before a vessel was washed it was necessary to observe whether or not it had a brim. Bowls with brims had to be immersed in washing; without brims it was not necessary. Certain cooking vessels were used for meat foods, others for milk foods. These pots could not be used interchangeably.

Many of the traditions were concerned with the Sabbath. The people were very rigid in their observance of the Sabbath. No work was permitted—but the problem was to determine what was work. They divided work into 39 classes, such as sowing, plowing, reaping, baking, and spinning. Under each of these heads there were many special classes.

A fire could not be lighted. No one could swat a fly on the Sabbath day, as that was hunting. No woman was permitted to comb her hair. A stick could not be pushed forward into the earth, for that was plowing, but it was all right to drag this same stick behind one's back. No one could walk more than a mile and two-fifths on the Lord's Day. This was commonly known as a Sabbath day's journey. To walk two miles was sin. There was constant debate whether or not a person might eat an egg laid on the Sabbath.

Children were not allowed to run or skip in play. Weaving was work, and forbidden: tying or untying knots or putting two threads together were weaving actions and therefore were also forbidden. But if a man could tie or untie a knot with one hand, that was not work. If a man was sick unto death he might receive help, but minute rules governed even the use of medicine and remedies. He who had a toothache must not rinse his mouth with vinegar (as a gargle), but he could wash his mouth with vinegar (that is, swallow it), for that would be like taking food. There was always danger in breaking the Sabbath rest.

CHAPTER SEVEN

Prophet and Priest

Because of the strong emphasis on religion in their culture, it is not strange that many of the Hebrew people were engaged in religious work. In order to appreciate the background of the Scripture it is necessary to know something about these religious occupations.

Prophets

The prophets were a special group of people called and chosen by God to declare His purposes. They were seers, servants of God, and interpreters of the divine will.

During the time of the judges, the priesthood sank into a state of degeneracy and the people were no longer influenced by the ceremonial service. A new moral power was evoked by the hand of God through the prophets. With a sensitive conscience and a deep communion with God, each prophet was given the power to protest against the social sins of his day. These men were the national poets of Judah. They were preachers of patriotism with a religious motive. They challenged the moral situation of the day with vehemence. They were exponents of the Law. But their greatest work was to reveal God's will to man often by predicting future events, and especially by telling of the Messiah and redemption through Him.

Joel, Obadiah, Micah, and Zephaniah were counted among the poets. Amos preached against the corruptions of Samaria. Jeremiah, Zechariah, Ezekiel, Daniel, Micah and many others predicted the coming of the Messiah and future events. Isaiah spoke against the religious and political iniquity of Jerusalem, but his greatest emphasis was the Messianic hope, fulfilled in Jesus.

The prophets lived in bands or schools. Samuel and his prophets lived at Ramah (I Sam. 19:19-20). Here he had a school to train young men to teach the law of God to the people. Most of the men who came to this school of the prophets were Levites. They studied the history and laws of Israel, poetry, and music. They were given mental and spiritual training so they could exert an influence for good upon the people of their day. The writing of sacred history was an important part of the work of these prophets.

During the reign of King Saul there may have been a school for prophets at Gibeah, as Samuel mentions "a company of prophets" there (I Sam. 10:5, 10). "Fifty men of the sons of the prophets" lived at Jericho (II Kings 2:5, 7). Elijah and Elisha lived at Gilgal (II Kings 4:38). The greatest of the prophets was Jesus, who was the fulfillment of all prophecy.

In the New Testament the term prophet refers to preachers or evangelists. They were Christian teachers to whom the Spirit, at times, made special direct communication though of minor importance. They interpreted God's will to man. Agabus was a prophet of Jerusalem (Acts 11:27-28). The four unmarried daughters of Philip of Caesarea prophesied (Acts 21:9).

Priests

Priests were the most influential members of the society in Bible lands. They were the holiest of the religious leaders, entrusted with the sacrifices at the temple in Jerusalem. They became the representatives of the people in things pertaining to God. Under the patriarchal system, the head of the family acted as the priest.

The priesthood was first established as an order at the time of Moses. This priestly order was hereditary. Aaron, his sons, and their descendants were separated forever, to the office of the priesthood, from all other Israelites. The first-born son of Aaron succeeded him in office, and the elder son among all his descendants. Priests were required to prove their descent from Aaron.

The dress they wore during their ministrations consisted of linen drawers and a close-fitting cassock. This cassock was gathered about the body with a girdle of needlework. Upon their heads they wore a cap or bonnet in the form of a cup-shaped flower. They were always barefooted when they ministered at the altar. Before they went into the tabernacle they were required to wash their hands and feet.

Their chief duties were to watch over the fire on the altar of burnt offerings and to keep it burning at all times. They were to feed the golden lamp outside the veil with oil so it would not go out. They offered the morning and evening sacrifices. They were to teach the children the law of God. Sometimes they acted as a court of appeals in controversies.

Priests were supported by a tenth of the tithes paid to the Levites (Num. 18:26-28). They were also given a part of the spoils of war (Num. 31:25-47). They received the showbread, and the meat of the burnt offerings, the peace offerings, and the trespass offerings (Num. 18:8-14).

The priests were divided into 24 "courses" or orders (I Chron. 24:1-9) each of which served for one week. Zechariah, the father of John the Baptist, was serving with his division when the angel came to announce the birth of a son (Luke 1:8). The assignment of special services for the week was determined by lot (Luke 1:9). Each course began their work on the Sabbath at the evening sacrifices (II Chron. 23:8).

When the priests were not serving at the temple they acted as teachers (II Chron. 15:3). Others served as interpreters of the Law. Many of the priests devoted themselves to study and were given a special call to become a prophet. Some became careless, lazy, tyrannical, and addicted to drink (Isa. 28:7-8).

The priests who lived at Jerusalem dwelt in large palaces and had enormous staffs to assist them. It has been estimated that 27,000 priests lived in Jerusalem and 1200 at Jericho. Thus it would be quite natural for a priest to go down the Jericho road (Luke 10:31). The priests were permitted to enter the holy place of the temple to offer sacrifices at the appointed times. They also handled the sacred treasuries. Priests were selected for their physical fitness and good character.

High Priests

Aaron was selected to be the first high priest and was anointed for this special task (Lev. 8:12). The dress of the high priest consisted of eight garments. The breastplate was set with 12 precious stones, one for each of the 12 tribes of Israel. Each stone had the name of one of the sons of Israel engraved upon it. The second part of the high priest's garb was the ephod. This consisted of two parts, which covered the breast and back of the body. These were clasped together on the shoulder with two large onyx stones. The ephod was held together at the waist with a linen girdle of gold, blue, purple, or scarlet.

The robe was the third part of the high priestly garb. Of poorer material than the ephod, it was blue in color and worn under the ephod. The blue robe had no sleeves. The skirt of this robe was trimmed in pomegranates of blue, red, and crimson, with a bell of gold. The bell clanged as the priest walked in and out of the holy place.

The miter was a turban worn on the head. It had a gold plate inscribed with the words, "Holiness to the Lord." The fifth article of clothing for the high priest was the embroidered coat. This was a long skirt or tunic of linen. The girdle was also of linen and was twisted around the body several times. The breeches or drawers were of linen and covered the loins and thighs. The bonnet was a turban of linen. It partly covered the head.

The high priest was the supreme ruler of the people. He was always present when a new leader or ruler was appointed. He interceded with God for the rulers of the people. He had general charge of the sanctuary. Only he could enter the Most Holy Place.

Levites

The Levites were entrusted with the care of the property of the temple. Their position originated in the days of Moses; they were chosen from the tribe of Levi. They were not to begin their work until they were 30 years of age (Num. 4:23), and at the age of 50 they were freed from all duties except that of supervising the work (Num. 8:25-26). In the wilderness they cared for the tabernacle. When the Israelites moved, the Levites carried the ark and the vessels of the sanctuary (Num. 3:31).

The Levites did not inherit any part of the Promised Land, hence, they owned no property nor could they cultivate any land. They were, however, given 48 cities, with meadowland for flocks and herds (Num. 35:2, 7). They were supported by the offerings paid to them by the people. In a sense these Levites were the temple police or the "go-betweens" for the priests and the laity. Many of their members served in the Sanhedrin and had a share in the administration of justice. It was their duty to chant in the temple choir and to take part in the great processionals.

Scribes

The task of the scribes was to interpret the law. Ezra was the first scribe (Ezra 7:6). He introduced a new set of sacred rules from Babylon which were called the "priestly code." The exiles had developed a great reverence for the Law and were anxious to preserve the sacred books, the laws, hymns, and prophecies of the past. The office of the scribe thus became very prominent. However, as the scribes grew in importance they became arrogant, hungry for compliments, and jealous of their position in the Sanhedrin. They were domineering in the synagogues. Scribes also served as teachers of law, gathering about them pupils whom they compelled to memorize the sacred Law.

The scribes became expert copyists of the Scripture and interpreters of the same. They devoted themselves to a careful study of the text and laid down rules for copying it with scrupulous precision. They tried to make the Law of Moses the rule of life for the whole nation, but they perverted it so that the right relation of moral and ceremonial laws was absolutely inverted.

Soon the word of the scribes was honored above the Law. It became a greater crime to offend against the scribes than against the Law. They began to annul the commandments of God for the sake of their tradition. They began to tamper with the conscience and to evade the plainest duties (Matt. 15:1-6). Jesus poured out His greatest condemnation against them (Matt. 23:1-36). He called them hypocrites, whited sepulchres, offspring of vipers, blind guides, and extortioners. The scribes retaliated by endeavoring with the help of the priests to put Jesus to death (Luke 22:2).

Lawyers

The title "lawyer" is generally supposed to be equivalent to the title "scribe." Matthew speaks of a man as a lawyer while Mark in his Gospel calls the same man a scribe (Matt. 22:35, Mark 12:28). Titus refers to a lawyer as an interpreter of the law, a jurist (Titus 3:13). A man might be both a lawyer and a scribe, but this does not mean that all lawyers were scribes. It has been suggested that scribes were public expounders of the law while the lawyers were private expounders and teachers of it. The lawyers often tried to corner Jesus on matters of law. They were in turn condemned by Jesus for binding heavier burdens on others than they themselves were willing to bear.

Doctors of the Law

The Doctors of the Law were able jurists who specialized in the sacred statutes (Luke 5:17). They concerned themselves with teaching rather than with giving written opinions. They were mostly from the sect of the Pharisees, but were distinguished as a separate class of people (Luke 5:17). Gamaliel was probably the most famous person in this class (Acts 5:34).

Pharisees

The Pharisees were really a society rather than a sect. Their principal concern was to uphold the ancient customs and traditions of Judaism. There is no reference in the Old Testament to the Pharisees; however, they were very prominent at the time of Jesus. Josephus, the Jewish historian, refers to them as existing about 150 years before Christ. Thus they must have been prominent in the period between the two Testaments.

They were the strictest religious sect of their day. They were separated from the ordinary people by their careful observance of the rituals, laws, and ceremonies of their religion. They were extremely nationalistic and often used their power for political purposes. The Pharisees protested vigorously against anything that was non-Jewish. Therefore they tended to be very uncharitable about the observation of the laws and regulations of the Jewish religion. They adhered to the very last jot and tittle of the law, and were anxious to maintain their traditions at all costs.

Most of these men were proud of their religious orthodoxy. They were very severe in their punishments for any infraction of religious law, and tried to give their fellow men the impression that they were highly favored of God. Thus they became known for their shocking hypocrisy (Matt. 23:23,27), for which Jesus bitterly denounced them. Concerned only with the external observances of the religious life (Matt. 23:3), they became proud and arrogant. Often they were in reality fond of pleasures, and were men of lax morals (Matt. 23:3) who were not above stooping to shameful acts and vices. How they loved places of honor and rank (Matt. 23:5)! Of course, not all Pharisees were like this; some were upright and pure-minded men.

The Pharisees carefully avoided contamination. They

could not buy from or sell to anyone but a member of their order, nor have social dealings with anyone outside of their group. Any meat slaughtered by a Gentile was unclean and unfit to eat. They were careful to avoid defilement by even as much as touching a Gentile. They wore long fringes on their robes in order to show that they were separate from other Jews, and prayed long prayers in public places to be heard by men.

The headquarters for this sect was in Jerusalem, but they seemed to be found in every part of the country. There were about 6,000 of them in Jesus' day. They were bitterly opposed to Jesus. Their most concerted efforts at this time were to destroy the influence and teachings of the Messiah. They hated the Gospel message, and wielded tremendous power against the early Christian church. They constituted such a large portion of the Sanhedrin that any decision about Jesus or the church was bound to be unfavorable.

Sadducees

In contrast to the Pharisees, the Sadducees cared nothing about tradition. They came into power quite naturally as a reaction to the legalism of the Pharisees. They were determined to investigate and re-evaluate the prevalent customs and practices of the Pharisees. Thus they ended up in skepticism, rejecting many of the established practices of the Hebrew religion. It is not certain when this group came into being. However, they must have been organized as soon as the Pharisees became obnoxious, probably during the time of Alexander the Great. They never became a very large group. Some served in the Sanhedrin (Acts 23:6), and a few of the high priests came from this party. They disappeared suddenly from history after the first century.

They were an aristocratic, priestly party; they did not

believe in a personal resurrection from the dead, in spirits, or in angels (Acts 23:8). They were in reality the
modernists and freethinkers of their day. They, too, opposed Jesus because of His claims to the Messiahship,
which they feared might menace their own power. Only
on one recorded occasion did Jesus denounce this group
(Matt. 16:1-4). In politics, the Sadducees sided with the
Roman rulers, and had little to do with the ordinary
people.

Rabbis

"Rabbi" was a title of dignity and honor that the
Hebrew people gave their doctors and teachers of the
law. It signified that the person was a master or teacher.
The title "rabbi" was not known to have been used be-
fore the rule of Herod the Great. During the time of
Jesus a rabbi usually presided over the temple.

The disciples and followers of Jesus often used the
term in addressing their Master. The highest title of all
was "Rabboni" which implies, "my great Master." This
was used by Mary when she discovered her risen Savior
(John 20:16).

Herodians

The Herodians were a class of Jews that existed at the
time of Jesus. It is not easy to determine whether they
were a religious or a political group. The New Testament refers to them in connection with the religious
groups that opposed Jesus. They favored the Roman
government and opposed the Jews who were hostile to
Rome. They wanted to better their social and political
standing by taking a stand for Roman domination.

The Herodians joined with the Pharisees in a plot to
destroy Jesus (Mark 3:6). They came to entrap Jesus by
the question, "Is it lawful to pay taxes to Caesar, or
not?" (Mark 12:14.)

Essenes

Although this religious group is not mentioned in the Bible, they were a sect that flourished in Jesus' day. Their sole purpose was to achieve a standard of absolute holiness. They were ascetics who lived in austere simplicity. They gladly deprived themselves of the luxuries and niceties of life in order to attain to purity and holiness. Ordinary pleasures were avoided as something that was morally bad. They despised marriage. They lived as a brotherhood in communities which were regulated by strict rules. All property was held in common. They were generous in the care of the poor. Self-denial, temperance, and agricultural labor were the marks of the life of the Essenes. They opposed slavery, war, and commerce. Buying and selling were unknown among them.

It is thought that John the Baptist was a member of this religious sect. They had a settlement along the northwest shore of the Dead Sea. The Dead Sea scrolls are thought to be a part of the library of the Essenes. Under the attack of enemies, the scrolls were hidden in clay pots in a cave by the seashore.

Samaritans

The Samaritans are really a race of people rather than a religious profession. Yet one cannot read of the scribes, Pharisees, Sadducees, and Levites without meeting the Samaritans. They were a people who came into being as a result of the Assyrian invasions of Palestine. The important people of Israel were carried away into Assyria into captivity (II Kings 17:5-6). The poor, the feeble, and the inconsequential Israelites were left behind in the Holy Land in desolation.

King Shalmaneser brought in people from Babylon,

Cuthah, Avva, Hamath, and Sepharvaim to populate the
devastated area (II Kings 17:24). These people carried
along with them their own idolatrous religion. The Israelites left in Palestine intermarried with the heathen
who were brought into this country by Assyria. Thus they
became a mixed race with a mixed religion and were
known as Samaritans.

When the Jews returned from the Babylonian captivity
to rebuild Jerusalem, these mixed Jews, or Samaritans,
came to join in the rebuilding of the temple. The Jews
refused help from these folks because they were now
ceremonially unclean as a result of intermarriage with
the pagan Gentiles. Thereupon the Samaritans became
open enemies of the Jews. They did everything in their
power to annoy the returned exiles.

This bitterness between the Jews and the Samaritans
grew in intensity up through the New Testament era.
Orthodox Jews refused to walk through Samaria on their
way from Galilee to Judea. They purposely walked on
the other side of the Jordan River so as not to contami-
nate themselves by walking among the Samaritans. This
deep hatred gives the real significance to Jesus' parable
of the "Good Samaritan."

The Samaritans built their own temple on Mt. Gerizim
in Samaria. A son of the Jewish high priest, Manasses,
joined their ranks because of his marriage to a daughter
of the Samaritan governor. He organized the religious
life of these people. They accepted only the first five
books of the Old Testament as their code. The woman at
the well in Samaria called Jacob "our father" (John 4:
12). Jews who gave up their religion often came to
Samaria to join their ranks.

The Samaritan's strange religion and mixed blood
have continued up to this day. At the present time there
are only a few hundred Samaritans left in this interesting

colony in central Palestine. Shechem, now called Nabulus, is their present center. They still worship on Mt. Gerizim.

Gentiles

The Gentiles are referred to many times in the New Testament. It was a term applied by the Hebrews to all foreigners or strangers who were not Jewish. It was synonymous with pagan or heathen. All nations of the world except Jews were Gentiles.

Proselytes

Proselytes were Gentiles who adopted the Jewish religion and carefully observed all the laws and regulations of their new faith. No stranger could become a Jew unless he accepted the entire law (Exod. 12:48, Num. 15:15). However, a proselyte was never permitted to enter certain areas of the temple because of his Gentile background. The Pharisees were very zealous to make proselytes. Jesus rebuked them for their false motives (Matt. 23:15). Most of the proselytes were women.

CHAPTER EIGHT

Daily Work

POTTER'S WHEEL

The Biblical writers had varied backgrounds, and in their writing they make allusions to many different occupations or skills. A knowledge of the Hebrew trades and professions is very helpful in understanding what many of these references mean.

Craftsmen in the Orient showed remarkable skill in the use of simple tools and produced excellent workmanship with rude instruments. The father's occupation was generally adopted by the son, from generation to generation. Sometimes the family developed trade secrets which were closely guarded. The artisan took great pride in his work and developed his trade into a skill.

The Potter

The making of pottery was one of the most important trades of Bible lands. Large jars were needed to carry water and to store oil, honey, and meal. Vessels of copper and bronze were very expensive; leather was unsatisfactory. Thus, there was a real demand for clay pottery. Moreover, since clay jars broke easily, it was necessary to replace them constantly.

The clay used in making these pots was trodden underfoot until it was the right consistency. Isaiah spoke of this treading of the clay (Isa. 41:25). When this was done the potter brought the clay into his crude workshop where the potter's wheel stood by a heavy wooden bench.

The potter's wheel consisted of two flat, wooden wheels, the upper one supported on an axle or wooden stick standing up from the center of the lower disc. The lower wheel was put into action by the foot. This in turn began spinning the upper wheel in a horizontal motion. A small lump of clay was put on this revolving upper wheel. As the wheel turned, the soft clay was shaped into a conelike vessel. The thumb was used to make a hole in the top of the whirling clay. This opening was widened until it was the desired size of the jar wanted. If necessary, water was sprinkled on the clay to keep it moist and pliable. A small piece of wood in the right hand was used to smooth the outside of the vessel. This was also used to give the pottery a grooved or rough surface if that was desired. Jeremiah spoke of the potter's wheel (Jer. 18:3).

Sometimes the vessel would not have the desired

shape, or it might be marred in the process of shaping. The potter then crushed the vessel into a lump, softened it with water, and began again. Jeremiah described this process in speaking of God's right to change His course of action (Jer. 18:4). Paul too said, "Has the potter no right over the clay, to make

POTTER'S KILN

out of the same lump one vessel for beauty and another for menial use?" (Rom. 9:20-21).

The finished vessels were put on a shelf, protected from the sun but open to the wind, so that they would slowly set in shape. When a sufficient number of jars had been prepared they were put in a small circular kiln or oven. The fire hardened the clay to make it fairly strong. Some of the pottery was glazed before baking (Prov. 26:23). However, water jars were left unglazed, so that the process of evaporation would keep the water cool.

This type of pottery was very brittle and broke easily. No wonder the Bible writers compared God's divine judgment to the "breaking of a vessel." "You shall dash them in pieces like a potter's vessel" (Ps. 2:9). "So will I break this people and this city, as one breaks a potter's vessel, so that it can never be mended" (Jer. 19:11).

Even the broken pieces of pottery were often used by the people. These fragments were called potsherds. Isaiah said:

And its breaking is like that of a potter's vessel which is smashed so ruthlessly that among its fragments not a sherd is found with which to take fire from the hearth, or to dip up water out of the cistern (Is. 30:14).

These potsherds were used in carrying hot coals, in draining a pit, as ladles in filling vessels, and as drinking cups. The sherds were also used in recording memoranda of business transactions. Job scraped his sores with a potsherd (Job 2:8).

POTSHERDS

Many such fragments have been uncovered by the archaeologists. Pottery has been very helpful in archaeological discoveries. It forms the basis on which the chronology of a city or civilization can be determined. Each culture in history has had its own distinctive type of pottery. The trained eye of an archaeologist can distinguish to which age the pottery belonged. This has been very helpful in dating the strata or remains of the homes and civilization of Bible land people.

The Carpenter

The work of the carpenter was done at his bench. Isaiah mentions four tools that were used by this artisan. "The carpenter stretches a line, he marks it out with a pencil; he fashions it with planes, and marks it with a compass" (Isa. 44:13). The line was no doubt a crude rule used to measure lengths. This rule was in reality a measuring reed which was six times a cubit, plus a handbreadth, or from ten to eleven feet (Ezek. 40:5). The measuring line was 146 feet (Zech. 2:1). The pencil was probably a simple stylus used in making marks on clay tablets. The plane would smooth the lumber, and the compass was an instrument for making a circle.

In Deuteronomy we read of the axe that was used to cut down the timber (Deut. 19:5). The awl was in common use at that time (Exod. 21:6). They used a saw made from sharp flint stones placed in a row. Later saws were made from thin pieces of metal (Isa. 10:15). Jeremiah referred to the use of hammer and nails (Jer. 10:4). David prepared iron for nails to be used in the building of the temple (I Chron. 22:3). Solomon used golden nails in the temple (II Chron. 3:9).

These rough tools were used to make yokes for the oxen, plows, tables, chairs, benches, chests, wooden locks,

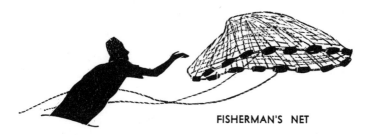

FISHERMAN'S NET

keys, and sandals. The carpenter was called upon to
make a wooden sledge for the threshing floor, and
crude frames for the doors and windows, and to lay
beams to support the earthen roofs of buildings.

The Fisherman

Fishing was an important vocation of Bible land people. Bethsaida on the northern shore, where the Jordan
River entered, and the other Bethsaida near Capernaum
were the best fishing places on the Sea of Galilee. The
Mediterranean Sea furnished much fishing for those who
lived along its coast. The Bible speaks of the Nile
River as being a good fishing ground. In the wilderness the Israelites remembered the "fish we ate in
Egypt" (Num. 11:5).

Hooks were used for catching fish. Peter used a hook
to catch the fish in which he found a coin to pay the
temple tax (Matt. 17:27). Isaiah said, "The fishermen
will mourn and lament all who cast hook in the
Nile" (Isa. 19:8). Amos spoke of this also when he said,
"They shall take you away with hooks, even the last of
you with fishhooks" (Amos 4:2). Archaeologists have discovered such fishhooks in Galilee.

Another method of catching fish was referred to by
Job. "Can you fill his skin with harpoons, or his **head**

with fishing spears?" (Job 41:7.) Thus the custom of
fishing is very old.

A third means of catching fish was through the use
of nets. Peter and Andrew were casting nets into the
sea when Jesus met them and called them to be his
disciples (Mark 1:16-17). Miller and Miller in their book,
Encyclopedia of Bible Life, describe this kind of net:

This casting net was draped over the arm of the fisherman
who stood on the shore or waded into the water. This net
was skillfully whirled around and allowed to fall in a teal
shape or cone; its lead weights pulled it to the bottom so
that it would enclose the fish.*

These nets were always washed after they were used,
and hung out in the sun to dry. The fishermen had to
keep constant watch so that rips and tears were mended
immediately. James and John were mending their nets
when Jesus called them (Matt. 4:21-22).

Jesus spoke of the dragnet which was "thrown into
the sea and gathered fish of every kind; when it was
full, men drew it ashore and sat down and sorted the
good into vessels but threw away the bad" (Matt. 13:47-
48). This was a type of seine which had floats on the top
and weights on the bottom. Sometimes these nets were
worked with two boats, especially out in deep waters.

The Mason

Masonry was always an important work among the
people of the Bible. Masons were clever in shaping
stones and building arches. The plumb line was used
to insure a perpendicular wall. Amos spoke of this instrument: "Behold, I am setting a plumb line in the
midst of my people Israel" (Amos 7:8). This was simply
a small piece of metal or stone fastened on the end of

---

*Miller, Madeleine and Lane, *Encyclopedia of Bible Life* (Harper
& Brothers, New York, 1944), p. 346.

a line. When suspended from the top, the line would just barely touch the wall. This was a guide for laying successive layers of stone and brick.

Ezekiel spoke of a "measuring reed" (Ezek. 40:3), which was a cane used by the mason to lay the foundations of the walls in a straight line and to measure the spaces between the doors and windows.

The first task of a mason was to dig a deep, wide trench. Into this, stone and lime were packed for the foundation. Jesus told of the good mason who "dug deep, and laid the foundation upon rock" (Luke 6:48). When the first layer of stone was laid above the foundation, a large square stone was set at each corner to bind the walls together (Job 38:6).

Similarly, a thin square stone was often placed at the top of each corner to bind the top course of stones together. This was the head of the corner. A stone rejected as too thin for the main wall was often found to be just the right stone for this purpose. Thus Jesus was referred to as the stone which the builders rejected, yet He became the chief cornerstone (Matt. 21:42).

The Metal Worker

Metal workers appear early in the Scriptures. "Tubal-cain, the forger of all instruments of bronze and iron," is mentioned in the fourth chapter of Genesis (Gen. 4:22). Thus in the first generations after Adam, men had learned the use of metal crafts.

In the days of King Saul the Philistines placed a ban on Hebrew blacksmiths. "Now there was no smith to be found throughout all the land of Israel; for the Philistines said, 'Lest the Hebrews make themselves swords or spears'" (I Sam. 13:19). Jewish blacksmiths were active in the days of Isaiah, for he said, "The iron-smith fashions it and works it over the coals; he shapes

**FORKS, PICKAXE
AND GOAD**

it with hammers" (Isa. 44:
12). Isaiah also referred to
the blacksmith's "anvil"
which was a cube of iron
fixed upon a block of wood
(Isa. 41:7). Jeremiah mentioned the "bellows" made
of the undressed skin of a
goat, and usually worked
by the foot of the workman
(Jer. 6:29).

The blacksmith made the
plowshare, mattock (a sort
of pickaxe or hoe), axe, fork, and goad. When the Lord
spoke to Saul on the Damascus road, He said, "It hurts
you to kick against the goads" (Acts 26:14). This goad
was a rod about eight feet long, brought to a sharp
point and sometimes cased with iron at the head. It was
used to urge on the oxen (Judg. 3:31).

When King Solomon built the temple he engaged
workers to build the vessels, the pots, the shovels, and
the basins of bronze (I Kings 7:45). Nehemiah spoke of
"goldsmiths" (Neh. 3:8). Paul's missionary work in
Ephesus was hindered by silversmiths who made images
of the goddess Artemis (Acts 19:23-27). Peter spoke of
the goldsmith's task in relation to the Christian life, say-
ing that faith, "more precious than gold which though
perishable is tested by fire" (I Peter 1:7), is also tested.

The Tanner

Peter stayed in the house of Simon, "a tanner," while
he was at Joppa (Acts 9:43). The tanning of skins and
hides of animals was an important industry among these
people. Goatskins were used in making bottles to carry
water, to hold new wine, and to store milk. These goatskin bags were often used as churns to make butter.

The holes of the legs and tail were sewn up and the neck opening served as the top of the bottle. Jesus spoke of the wine bag in connection with His denunciation of the Pharisees (Mark 2:22). Sheepskin was used in the making of shoes. Many articles of clothing were made from leather, tanned and prepared by the tanner.

The Dyer

Dyeing was another industry of the Hebrews. Purple was made from a secretion of shellfish. It was very valuable because only one drop was found in each fish. Thus purple became the "royal" color for kings and their nobles. Lydia, "a seller of purple," was the first Christian convert in Europe (Acts 16:14). Blue came from the rind of the pomegranate. The dye for brilliant crimson came from a grub that fed on the oak and other plants.

The various colored dyes were put in large stone vats and the cloth or yarn was soaked in them. When it was sufficiently colored, the dyer would wring out the surplus dye; then the color was set by soaking for a time in a lime mixture.

The Tentmaker

Because of the general use of tents by the Hebrew people, the making of tents was also an important industry. The material for making the tent came from the coarse black hair of goats. Priscilla and Aquila were tentmakers; Paul worked with them in Corinth (Acts 18:1-3). He used aprons in the shop of Aquila in his work as a tentmaker (Acts 19:12).

The Merchant

The market place was important in the lives of these people. Here the merchants applied their trade. These places were usually near the gate, or in the open squares in the center of the city. Often certain streets were set aside for some particular trade or merchandise. Jeremiah spoke about the "bakers'" street (Jer. 37:21).

Often goods were bartered rather than being sold for money. Sometimes metals were weighed out in payment of a commodity. Thus Abraham "weighed out for Ephron the silver which he had named in the hearing of the Hittites" for the purchase of the cave of Machpelah (Gen. 23:16). Often there was no set price for an article, so there was much argument and haggling. When the sale was made, the buyer walked away boasting of the good bargain he had made. The Book of Proverbs pictures such a person, "'It is bad, it is bad,' says the buyer; but when he goes away, then he boasts" (Prov. 20:14).

Many times credit was used. Jesus tells of the unjust steward who tried to collect "a hundred measures of oil" and "a hundred measures of wheat" (Luke 16:5-7). A bushel measure was used for measuring grain. The measure, however, was to be "pressed down and running over" (Luke 6:38).

The Money Changer

The money changer was a familiar sight in every village and city. He would sit by a table in a conspicuous place to change the people's money from one type of currency to another. Interest was charged for the transaction. Sometimes this was unfair and expensive.

In the temple the money changers were busy, because the temple tax of a half shekel had to be paid by every male Israelite who was 21 years of age or over. This had to be paid in the exact Hebrew coin called the half shekel. Many of these people were from distant countries and used a different system of coinage. Thus it was necessary to go to the money changer to get the right and

accepted coin. A rate of about 12 per cent was charged
for this according to the Hebrew Talmud. These money
changers were also necessary to provide the exact coins
with which to purchase the doves, lambs, or whatever the
family offered as a sacrifice. This business was unscrupu-
lous and was held in ill repute by the people.

By the law of Moses the Israelites were forbidden to
accept interest on loans of money to their brethren (Lev.
25:36-37). Interest could be taken from strangers and
Canaanites, however (Deut. 23:20). In the New Testament a reasonable interest could be charged (Matt.
25:27). Jesus denounced all extortion or excessive interest rates (Luke 6:35).

The Banker

In the parable of the talents, Jesus implied that there
were bankers in His day. "Why then did you not put
my money into the bank, and at my coming I should
have collected it with interest?" (Luke 19:23)

The Tax Collector

The tax collector, sometimes called a publican, was
not a very popular person. His task was legitimate
enough, as taxes had to be collected in order to run the
government. However, resentment came because he collected the taxes for the foreign Roman government.
Roman officials employed Jews who were willing to
profit at the expense of their countrymen to collect the
taxes. There was much graft in connection with the collection of this money. The publicans of Jesus' day were
always designated as "sinners" (Matt. 9:11). They were
also classed with "harlots" (Matt. 21:31). Certain men
gave Jesus the title, "friend of publicans and sinners,"
because He was concerned about their souls (Matt.
11:19). In fact Jesus called Matthew, a publican, to be

His disciple (Mark 2:14). Zacchaeus was another famous publican (Luke 19:2).

The Physician

There were physicians in Bible times. The first ones, however, were simply magicians, though they had some practical ability such as plugging the nose in case of hemorrhage. Dipping in the Jordan River seems to have been advocated as a cure for leprosy. Washing in the Pool of Siloam was looked upon as a cure-all. Boils were treated with a plaster of hot figs (II Kings 20:7). Spas with hot baths were also recommended for healing diseases.

Job talked of "worthless physicians" (Job 13:4); and Mark wrote of the poor woman who "suffered much under many physicians" (Mark 5:26). But Jeremiah cried out, "Is there no physician there?" (Jer. 8:22). Paul calls Luke the "beloved physician" (Col. 4:14). Luke was well trained in the medical knowledge of his day. Most of this training took place in Greece.

The greatest physician of all times, of course, was Jesus. The Gospels are filled with cures that He wrought by the sheer power of the Word and prayer.

The Day Laborer

In every city there were many people who worked by the day. They gathered in the public market places to seek employment (Matt. 20:3-4). Some of these people served as porters, who carried heavy loads from place to place. Others were mason's assistants, who carried the stones from the quarry to the wall (Neh. 4:10). A few carried their pickaxe and hoe with them, ready to till the soil for those who needed such help. Many were willing to cut wood for the ovens. These day labor-ers stood in groups waiting to be hired for the day

(Deut. 24:15). If there was no employment, they and their families went hungry. Jesus spoke of the house-holder, "who went out early in the morning to hire laborers for his vineyard" (Matt. 20:1-16).

The Scribe

Aside from the religious scribe, there was also a pub-lic scribe who sat in front of the government build-ings, or on important street corners, with his inkhorn and parchment. His principal task was to write letters for those who could not write, to draw up contracts, and to make legal documents.

The Weaver

Weaving of cloth was an essential vocation of these people. Every home had a loom. Albert Bailey describes one of these looms in this way:

To make a loom, two stout posts were driven into the ground. Between these near the bottom was a horizontal roller to which the warp threads were fastened and on which the cloth was wound up as woven. The warp threads then went horizontally under another roller, up to the ceiling in the farther corner of the shop, and there were tied in a hank and weighted to keep the threads tight. The warp threads were alternated by two harnesses worked by treadles, and the shuttle containing the woof thread was thrown by hand from side to side. The operator sat on the floor with his feet in a pit where were the treadles. After a few shots with the shuttle the worker took a wooden "pin" shaped like a long blunt-edged knife, and with it beat the woven threads close together to make the cloth firm.*

The wool which was used came from their own flocks. It had to be spun into yarn without the use of modern spinning wheels. The women used the hand spindle.

---

*Bailey, Albert, *Daily Life in Bible Times* (Charles Scribner's Sons, New York, 1943), p. 191.

The spindle itself consisted of a thin wooden stick about a foot long; it had a notch at the top and was stuck through a whorl so that the weight came in the lower half. (These spindle whorls were made of stone, clay, or bone and their purpose was to weight the spindle shaft and give it momentum.) To do her work, the spinster held the strands of combed wool in her left hand, or under her left arm, and with the right hand drew out enough to twist into a yarn between her thumb and forefinger. She attached this yarn to the notch of her spindle, gave it a sharp twist, and then let it fall in front of her. As it fell, it gave a twist to the thread and when it got near the ground, she stopped it and wound the thread on to the spindle shaft.*

LOOM

This is spoken by the writer of the Book of Proverbs, who said, "She puts her hands to the distaff, and her hands hold the spindle" (Prov. 31:19). The distaff was a stick which held the combed wool. It was held in the left hand so the right hand was free to manipulate the thread and spindle. The women were so adept that they could spin the yarn as they walked, talked, or even ate in an informal way.

*Heaton, Eric W., *Everyday Life in Old Testament Times* (Charles Scribner's Sons, New York, 1956), p. 117.

DISTAFF

The Vinedresser

Vine culture was an important occupation of these outdoor people. The vineyards were usually located on hillsides. A retaining wall was built around the vineyard, and the hills were terraced by filling in earth from the valley. Each vine was trained in a separate stock, pruned back each season to the main stem, and propped up to keep the grapes above the soil. Nothing else was ever planted in the vineyard (Deut. 22:9). It took generations to build up these vineyards. Sometimes a briar hedge was planted beside the wall to keep out thieves (Isa. 5:5).

Every vineyard had a watchtower, built of field stones. Here the owner or vinedresser stayed during the harvest season to guard the grapes. There was also a winepress. This was hollowed out of solid limestone in the ground. The grapes were placed in it and the juice was trodden out by bare feet (Isa. 63:2). The juice ran into a vat hewn out on a lower level where it was allowed to settle; then the clear liquid was stored in jars of clay or goatskin bottles.

WINEPRESS

SOWING SEED

The Farmer

Grains were sown by hand as described so completely in the story of the Four Soils (Mark 4:3-8). The ground was made ready by crude wooden plows pulled by oxen. Those who had no oxen used the mattock or pick-axe to break up the soil and prepare the seed bed. The ripened grain was cut with a sickle. In early times sickles were made of flint, but in later periods iron was used. The women bound the grain into sheaves to be carried to the threshing floor. W. M. Thomson describes these threshing floors thus:

> The construction of the floor is very simple. A circular space, from 30 to 50 feet in diameter, is made level, if not naturally so, and the ground is smoothed off and beaten solid, that the earth may not mingle with the grain in the threshing.*

The most common method of threshing the grain was to pound it out with a flail. This was some kind of wooden instrument. We read that Ruth "beat out what she had gleaned" (Ruth 2:17). Gideon, too, "was beating out wheat in the winepress" (Judg. 6:11). A wooden sledge pulled by oxen was

THE REAPER

*Thomson, W. M., *The Land and the Book*, Vol. I (Baker House, Grand Rapids, Michigan, 1954), p. 151.

also used to beat out the grain.
Some of these sledges had stone
or metal teeth to assist in the
pulling out of the grain. Isaiah
described such a threshing instrument: "Behold, I will make
of you a threshing sledge, new,
sharp, and having teeth."

The wheat was separated from
the straw with a winnowing fork.
During a breeze, the grain was
thrown up into the air so that
the chaff would be blown to one
side and the ripe heads of grain
would fall directly to the ground

FLAIL AND
WINNOWING
FORK

(Ps. 1:4). John the Baptist spoke of the winnowing fork
in connection with the work of Jesus: "His winnowing
fork is in his hand, and he will clear his threshing floor
and gather his wheat into the granary, but the chaff he
will burn with unquenchable fire" (Matt. 3:12).

YOKE

OXEN AND PLOW

The Shepherd

Sheep were very common in the Holy Land. One of the chief responsibilities of the shepherd was to find food and water for the flock. In the springtime there was an abundance of green pasture. In late summer when the grain was gathered, the sheep would glean what was left in the fields. When dry weather came in the fall, the shepherd's task became difficult. Then the flocks were taken to the hill country where leafy branches were cut from the trees for the sheep to eat.

Water was a necessity. The shepherd hoped always to be near a running stream. When the pools and streams were dry the sheep were watered from a well. Sheep were watered at noon (Gen. 29:7).

The shepherd carried a long rod. This was a branch of a tree with a knot on the end. It was used for protection against wild animals and robbers. A sling was also used against lurking enemies. It was made of a string or piece of rope with a leather receptacle to hold a stone. This sling was swung around the head and then discharged by letting go of one of the strings.

The staff was a cane, five or six feet in length. It was used as a walking stick. Sometimes it was in the form of a crook. David spoke of these in his shepherd psalm: "Thy rod and thy staff, they comfort me" (Ps. 23:4). The shepherd's pipe was a flute of reed. The strange sounds which came from this instrument comforted the shepherd boy and aroused the attention of the sheep.

The sheepfold was a fence or corral built of tangled thorn bushes, branches of trees, rocks, or logs. This was a shelter for the sheep at night. They were often built on the sunny slopes of a hill so as to give protection from the cold. In one corner of the sheepfold was a roof to protect the sheep from snow and rain.

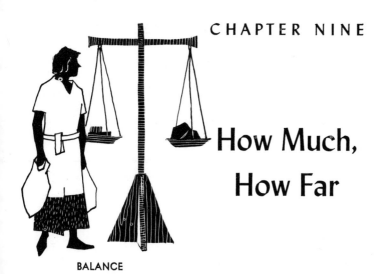

CHAPTER NINE

How Much, How Far

BALANCE

The leisurely life of plow-pulled Palestine was free from the tyranny of punctuality and engagement book. The Israelites were not much concerned about time. They used sundials (II Kings 20:9-11), but had little conception of fixed hours and minutes. They thought of time in relation to events. Thus when they wanted to refer to the fall of the year they called it "harvest time." The spring was "seed time."

They had names for months, but these were determined by a careful observation of the moon. These were lunar or "moon" months (Gen. 1:14). The commencement of the month was generally determined by observation of the new moon.

After the Babylonian exile the months were numbered from one to 12, beginning with the fall equinox. At first they were designated by their number only, as the "second month" (Gen. 7:11), or the "fourth month" (II Kings 25:3). Even after the months were named, the designation of numbers was retained, such as "in the

month of Ziv, which is the second month" (I Kings
6:1), and "in the third month, which is the month
Sivan" (Esther 8:9). The usual number of months was
12 (I Kings 4:7), but every third year an extra month
had to be added in order to keep in step with the
seasons. This extra month would be introduced seven
times in every 19 years. This month was called "Veadar."

The Jewish Year

The Jewish sacred year began in the spring with the
month Abib or Nisan. This was called the sacred year
since many of the feasts fell during this period. The
Passover came in Abib or Nisan. Pentecost, or the Feast
of Weeks, came during Sivan.

The civil year began in the autumn with the month
Ethanim or Tishri. Hence the Jewish New Year is in
the fall. The year was divided into two seasons, summer and winter. These are the only two seasons mentioned in the Bible. Summer was the time of cutting of
the fruits and winter was the time of gathering the
fruits. Thus these two seasons are really summer and
autumn according to our present seasons. They divided
the year into cold and warm periods.

The Sabbatical Year

Each seventh day and month were holy for the Israelites. Each seventh year was also a holy year and
called the Sabbatical year (Ex. 23:10-11). They were
to sow and reap the fields for six years, but during the
seventh year they were to let the land rest. There was
to be no tilling of the soil or cultivation of any sort during this year. The land was to lie fallow. During this
year all debts were remitted (Deut. 15:1-2).

The Year of Jubilee

The Year of Jubilee was the fiftieth year, following seven Sabbatical years. During this year all of the land which had been alienated from its owners was to be returned to the family to whom it originally belonged. All of the slaves of Jewish blood were to be set free (Lev. 25:8-16, 23-55).

This year began on the Day of Atonement with the blowing of the trumpets throughout the length and breadth of the land. The Jubilee year was observed until the destruction of Solomon's Temple.

The Calendar

1. Abib or Nisan	first month of the sacred year comparable to our March and April also called "latter" or "spring" rains the Passover comes in this month
2. Ziv or Iyar	second month of the sacred year comparable to our April and May
3. Sivan	third month of the sacred year comparable to May and June Pentecost or Festival of Weeks comes in this month.
4. Thammuz or Tammuz	fourth month of the sacred year comparable to June and July this month is not mentioned in the Bible the dry season

5. Ab

fifth month of the sacred year

comparable to July and August

this month is not mentioned in
the Bible

intense heat

6. Elul

sixth month of the sacred year

comparable to August and
September

the gathering of grapes

7. Ethanim or Tishri

first month of the civil year

seventh month of the sacred year

comparable to September and
October

the Day of Atonement and the
Feast of Tabernacles come in
this month

beginning of early rains

8. Bul or Marcheshvan

second month of the civil year

eighth month of the sacred year

comparable to October and
November

wheat and barley sown

9. Chisleu

third month of the civil year

ninth month of the sacred year

comparable to November and
December

Feast of Dedication comes in this
month

snow in mountains

10. Tebeth

fourth month of the civil year

tenth month of the sacred year

comparable to December and
January

11. Sebat or Shebat   fifth month of the civil year
                             eleventh month of the sacred year
                             comparable to January and
                               February
                             beginning of cold season

12. Adar   sixth month of the civil year
                             twelfth month of the sacred year
                             comparable to February and
                               March
                             Feast of Purim comes in this
                               month.

The Jewish Day

The day was reckoned from evening to evening (Lev. 23:32). The day was divided into morning, noon, and evening. The more precise indications of time were listed as dawn, sunrise, heat of the day, cool of the day, time when women went for water, and the evening sacrifice.

Later on in history, time was indicated by the hours of the day. Each day consisted of 12 hours, from sunrise to sunset (Matt. 20:1-12). The first hour was at 7 o'clock. Thus Jesus was crucified at the third hour which was 9:00 a.m. (Mark 15:25). It was the sixth hour or 12 o'clock noon when darkness came over the land (Mark 15:33). Jesus died at the ninth hour which was 3:00 p.m. (Mark 15:34).

The night was divided into watches from sunset to sunrise. The Israelites divided the night into three watches: the first was from sunset to midnight; the second, from midnight to cockcrow; and the third, from cockcrow to sunrise. The Romans divided the night into four watches. The first watch was from 6 to 9; the second, from 9 to 12; the third, from 12 to 3; and the fourth, from 3 to 6. Mark must have referred to the Roman

watches in telling the story of Jesus' walk upon the sea
(Mark 6:48).

The Jewish week consisted of seven days. Only the
Sabbath was given a name. The rest of the days were
simply numbered. Sunday was the first day of the week.

Weights

Knowledge of the weights used by the Hebrew people
is very limited and indefinite. These people had no interest in mathematics and definite reckonings. The sci-
ence of measurements was undeveloped among them.
Their weights and measures would vary from city to city.
Hence it is impossible to determine their system of
weights and measures with any degree of reliability.

The Balance

Isaiah cried out, "Who has . . . weighed . . . the hills
in a balance" (Isa. 40:12). Daniel interpreted the hand-
writing that appeared on a wall before Nebuchadnezzar in this way, "You have been weighed in the balances
and found wanting" (Dan. 5:27). The balance was in
common usage among the Israelites. Every person engaged in trade of any kind carried with him a pair of
balances or scales and a set of weights in a pouch or bag.
Dishonest men would carry two kinds of weights: the
lighter types for selling purposes, and the heavier
weights for buying (Micah 6:11).

The Shekel

Not until the time of Simon Maccabees do we have
any native Jewish coinage. The shekel and the half
shekel are the earliest Jewish coins known to exist.
These were made of silver and weighed 220 and 110

grains. This silver shekel was worth about 75 cents; the half shekel was worth about 38 cents. This half shekel was the coin used in the temple tax required of all men over 20 years of age (Exod. 30:11-16).

The Pound

Jesus told the parable of the Ten Pounds (Luke 19:13-23). He probably refers to the Greek pound which was valued at $16.50 to $17.00.

The Talent

This was the largest weight among the Israelites. In the Old Testament a talent of gold was worth about $55,000.00, while a talent of silver was valued at $2,250.-00. Jesus referred to this coin in the parable of the Unjust Steward (Matt. 18:23-25), and in the parable of the Talents (Matt. 25:14-30). In New Testament times the talent circulated in Palestine was probably worth $1,-550.00 to $2,000.00.

The Mite

The mite was a coin common in the Holy Land during the life of Jesus. It was probably the smallest piece of money. It was worth about two mills in American coinage.

The Farthing

There were two coins common in Palestine in the time of our Lord that were called by this name. One was valued at about 3.8 mills. Another farthing which was used had a value of one and one-half cents.

The Penny

This was a Roman silver coin valued at about 16 or 17 cents.

The Denarius

This coin is mentioned in the Feeding of the 5000 (Mark 6:37) and in the parable told by Jesus to Simon the Pharisee (Luke 7:41). It was equal in weight to the penny and worth about 16 or 17 cents.

The Stater

The stater was a Greek or Roman silver coin valued at about 50 cents.

The Piece of Silver

Jesus was betrayed by Judas for 30 pieces of silver, the price of a slave (Matt. 26:15). This piece of silver was probably equal to 35 cents. The coin in the parable of the woman who lost a piece of silver is probably a denarius, worth 17 cents (Luke 15:8-10).

Measures of Length

The Israelites took parts of the human body as their standards for the measurement of length. The finger, palm, and elbow were used.

THE FINGER

The finger was the smallest scale used in measurement among the Hebrews. It was equal to the breadth of a finger, or about three-fourths of an inch. The thickness of Solomon's pillars was measured by the finger (Jer. 52:21).

THE HANDBREADTH

This was a measurement of four fingers, or the breadth of the hand not including the thumb. This measurement was equal to about three and one-fourth

to three and one-half inches. The handbreadth was used
in many ways in the measurement of the temple (Exod.
37:12, I Kings 7:26). The Psalmist also refers to the
handbreadth as a measurement of the life span (Ps.
39:5).

THE SPAN

The measurement called the span was the distance
from the top of the little finger to the tip of the thumb,
stretched as far as possible. This would be about nine
and one-half inches. This measurement is used by Isaiah
(Isa. 40:12), and by Ezekiel in his measurement of the
altar (Ezek. 43:13).

THE CUBIT

The cubit was the measurement from the elbow to
the end of the middle finger. This distance would
equal about 18 inches. This was one of the most familiar measurements among the Hebrews. It was used
to describe the length of Noah's Ark (Gen. 6:14-16).
There are some indications that the cubit might have
varied. There was "the common cubit" (Deut. 3:11),
the "old standard" (II Chron. 3:3), and "a full reed
of six long cubits" (Ezek. 41:8).

THE PACE

The pace was equal to a step. It would correspond
to a yard or 36 inches (II Sam. 6:13).

THE FURLONG

Matthew used this term in recording the miracle of
Jesus walking on the sea (Matt. 14:24). The furlong
was a distance of about one-eighth of a mile. This was
a Greek form of measurement.

THE MILE

The Roman mile was 1612 yards in length. This was less than the mile used today of 5280 feet. The Jewish mile varied since it depended upon the pace used in different parts of the country (Luke 24:13, John 6:19).

THE SABBATH DAY'S JOURNEY

This distance was established when the Israelites went to look for manna in the wilderness on the seventh day. Moses asked everyone to "remain in his place" on that day (Exod. 16:29). This later became a permanent law. The distance allowed seems to have been based on the space to be kept between the Ark of the Covenant and the people in the wilderness (Josh. 3:4). The focal point of this measurement was the wall of the city to any distance outside the city. This distance measured 2000 paces or six furlongs in length. This would be equivalent to about one and two-fifths miles (Acts 1:12).

A DAY'S JOURNEY

This was the measurement used in figuring travel time. The term "a day's journey" did not indicate any definite length. It was the distance a person could normally travel in one day. The ordinary day's journey among the Hebrews was about 20 miles, but when they traveled in companies it was only ten miles. With a beast of burden the distance could be increased to 30 miles per day. (Gen. 30:36, Luke 2:44).

Measures of Capacity

The values of the liquid and dry measurements varied among the Israelites. It is therefore very difficult to give an exact estimate of this value.

THE DRY MEASUREMENTS

Dry measurements were used to measure grain, manna, and other dry substances. Some of the dry measurements were also used in determining the quantity of liquids. In selling grain in Bible lands it was the custom that each measure must run over. The grain was to be pressed down and then given two or three shakes to settle it well (Luke 6:38, Lev. 19:35-36).

> 1 kab—1-4/5 omer or 1 qt., 2/10 of a pt.
> 1 omer—3½ seahs or 2 qts.
> 1 seah—3 ephahs or 6 qts., 1½ pts.
> 1 ephah—10 homers or 3 pks., 3 pts.

THE HANDFUL

This measurement was the simplest. It was the capacity of a cupped hand (Lev. 2:2).

THE KAB

The kab is mentioned only once in the Bible (II Kings 6:25). It was equal to one-sixth of a seah or a little over one quart.

THE OMER

This measurement is also mentioned only in one part of the Bible, in connection with the gathering of the manna (Exod. 16:16-36). The word "omer" implies a heap or sheaf. It was one-tenth of an ephah. This was about two quarts.

THE BUSHEL

The bushel was a dry measure of moderate dimensions, amounting to about a peck (Mark 4:21). It was really a Roman measure but was also used by the Israelites.

THE SEAH OR MEASURE

The word seah means "measure." This was the ordinary measure used for household purposes. It was in very common use among the Hebrews. It was equal to one-third of an ephah and contained a little over six quarts.

THE EPHAH

The ephah was in general use among Bible land people. Ruth used the ephah to measure her gleanings (Ruth 2:17). The ephah contained about ten omers or three pecks and three pints. It was also equal to the bath in liquid measure.

THE HOMER

The homer contained ten ephahs or nearly eight bushels (Num. 11:32). The word really means "heap."

THE LIQUID MEASUREMENTS

The liquid and dry measurements were in some cases used interchangeably. There were only three liquid measures used.

$$1 \text{ log} = 1/12 \text{ of a hin or } 2/3 \text{ pt.}$$
$$1/72 \text{ of a bath}$$
$$1 \text{ hin} = 12 \text{ logs or } 3 \text{ qts., } 3/4 \text{ of a pt.}$$
$$1/6 \text{ of a bath}$$
$$1 \text{ bath} = 72 \text{ logs or } 5 \text{ gals., } 1 \text{ pt.}$$
$$6 \text{ hins}$$

THE LOG

This word means a hollow or a basin. It was equal to about one-twelfth of a hin. Its size was determined by the water displaced by six hens' eggs (Lev. 14:10). This was equal to about two-thirds of a pint.

THE HIN

The hin contained about 12 logs and held one-sixth of a bath, or three quarts and three-fourths of a pint, or a little over six pints (Ezek. 4:11).

THE BATH

This was the largest of the liquid measurements. It was equal to an ephah (three pecks and three pints). The bath contained six hins or about five gallons and one pint (I Kings 7:26).

BUSHEL

CHAPTER TEN

Teaching Traditions

The Israelites were not deeply concerned with education. They were not illiterate, yet they never excelled in book learning. They did not rise to great heights in literary culture like the civilizations of the Assyrians, Babylonians, Egyptians, or the Canaanites.

Informal Education

The Old Testament never mentions the word "school." Professional teachers as a class are not referred to until in the New Testament era. The average boy of Abraham's clan never went to school. However, Abraham himself was probably trained in his native city of Ur of the Chaldeans. In the ruins of this ancient city, archaeologists have discovered clay tablets showing a very high type of education. These tablets indicate that arithmetic, writing, and grammar were taught in the school. Thus Abraham probably learned to read and write as a boy. In his new home in Canaan, Abraham was not able to provide a formal education for his son and heirs. This was true even up to the time of Isaiah.

Moses, of course, was trained in the courts of Pharaoh in Egypt (Acts 7:22). The educational requirements of Egypt were of a high standard. Music, astronomy, architecture, anatomy, chemistry, and geometry were common subjects of learning. After leaving the court of Pharaoh, Moses was not able to provide his family and people with the formal education he had received as a boy.

The Mosaic law delegated the duty of education to the parents in the home. Thus Moses spoke the command of the Lord, "And these words which I command you this day shall be upon your heart; and you shall teach them diligently to your children, and shall talk of them when you sit in your house, and when you walk by the way, and when you lie down, and when you rise. And you shall bind them as a sign upon your hand, and they shall be as frontlets between your eyes. And you shall write them on the doorposts of your house and on your gates" (Deut. 6:6-9).

The father assumed the role of teacher and was responsible for the training of the boys. The mother was entrusted with the education and training of the girls. The home served as the school. There is some evidence to show that wealthy children may have had a special tutor. However, this was the rare exception and provided only an informal type of education for the upperclass children.

It is quite likely that only a small portion of the people was taught to read and write. Isaiah distinguished between the literate and the illiterate (Isa. 29:12). He also spoke of a child who could write (Isa. 10:19).

The Book of Proverbs stresses the importance of religious and moral instruction. It is doubtful if much of this instruction came from books. The Hebrew people relied a great deal on oral traditions. These traditions were handed down by word of mouth from father to son. Professional storytellers told the great stories of the national heroes of the Hebrews to the people gathered about them.

Formal Education

The tabernacle and the temple served as the first public schools for the Hebrews. Thus the priests and Levites became the first public school teachers for the Israelites. Whatever public training was available came in the worship on the Sabbath and feast days. Each seventh year at the Feast of Tabernacles, the entire Law was read to the people.

Under the priesthood of Eli and his evil sons, a new group of teachers came into being. These men were known as the prophets, and were led by Samuel. Special schools for training the prophets were established in several cities of Palestine. In these schools, music, poetry, Hebrew history, and law were taught.

The Synagogue School

The synagogue became an institution of the Hebrew religion during the time of the Babylonian captivity. While in Babylon they discovered that there was something worth learning outside of the Mosaic books. After the Jews returned to Palestine, synagogues soon sprang up everywhere and became the public schools for each community.

A graphic description of the synagogue in Nazareth in our Lord's day is given by an anonymous writer in these words:

(The schoolroom is) the interior of a squalid building, rudely constructed of stone, with a domed roof, and whitewashed walls, a wooden desk or cupboard on one side, and an inscription in Hebrew over the door. From the building, as we approach, comes the hum of many children's voices repeating the verses of the sacred Torah (the law) in unthinking and perfunctory monotone. The aged teacher sits silently in the midst. As we look in, we see his huge turban, his gray beard and solemn features, appearing over the ruddy faces of the dark-eyed boys who sit on the floor around him. The long row of tiny red slippers extends along the wall near the door. The earthen water bottle stands on the mat beside the Khazzan, or synagogue teacher. The scholars are the children of the richer members of the village community; . . . or "men of leisure," who form the representative congregation at every synagogue service; or of the "standing men" who go up yearly with the village priest for a week in Jerusalem to fulfill similar functions in the temple ritual.*

Between the age of five and six, all Hebrew boys began studying at this school to learn reading, writing and the Scriptures. They sat cross-legged in front of a very low desk. The girls, of course, never came to the synagogue school.

First of all the boys had to learn the Hebrew alphabet so that they could read and write in the language of the Law. "Aleph, beth, gimmel," the first letters of the Hebrew alphabet, were repeated after the rabbi until they were memorized. Then they continued until the entire alphabet was learned by heart. The recitation and studying were done out loud in shrill, monotonous, singsong voice. They studied many passages of Scripture until they could recite them from memory.

Some time after the boy was ten years old the law became the chief subject of study. Now the Book of Leviticus became the text. By the time a Jewish boy was 12 years of age he was supposed to know all of the laws and commandments. He would be held accountable for any infringement of the law. In other words he became a "son of the commandment" and took his right-

---

*Schaff-Herzog, *Encyclopedia of Religious Knowledge, Vol. II* (Funk & Wagnalls Company, New York) , p. 695.

ful place with the male members of the Jewish congregation. It was at this time that Jesus was "lost" in the temple.

Higher Education

Only a few Jewish boys continued their education beyond the synagogue school. Advanced education, however, was available for those who had the money and prestige necessary for such an education. The laws of the Jewish religion were so stringent and minute in detail that they provided endless opportunity for study. Paul came all the way from Tarsus to Jerusalem to study at the rabbinical school of Gamaliel. He graduated from this school to be a Pharisee (Acts 22:3). In the court of the temple there were places where the learned rabbis also taught these advanced students. These schools constituted the Hebrew university.

The Signature

People who could not write used scribes to do their letter writing. Business transactions were signed by a mark or signet ring. Job spoke of his signature in this way (Job 31:35). A more common way of signing a document was to use a seal. Jeremiah sealed a deed of purchase when he bought some property in his native village (Jer. 32:10-14). Sometimes when an Israelite borrowed money, he gave a garment in pledge. This was probably a symbol of indebtedness by the illiterate.

Writing Materials

Papyrus was the common writing material of this period. It is from the word "papyrus" that we get our word "paper" today.

Erich W. Heaton describes the process of making paper in this way:

Papyrus sheets for writing were made out of strips of the stem of the reed, first laid out in a row covering an area the size of the sheet required and then overlaid with cross strips. The two layers were then moistened, hammered out flat and dried in the sun. The off-white writing surface (the upper one with the cross strips) was finally smoothed with some hard substance such as ivory or shell. Sometimes the papyrus was used in single sheets, measuring about ten by six inches; sometimes the sheets were glued or sewn together to form a roll about 30 feet long. The two ends of the roll were sometimes attached to handles to make winding and unwinding easier; it must, nevertheless, have been extremely tedious when you wanted to look up a passage in a hurry.*

Bound books, in our present day form, did not come into use until the Christian era.

Animal skins were tanned in a special way and were used as a medium for writing important documents. Clay tablets were common in most civilizations. Tablets of wood were also used. Potsherds or broken pieces of pottery were often used as a media for short letters and business transactions. Today these are called "ostraca" and are very valuable in the study of archaeology.

Instruments for Writing

Ink was in evidence at an early age. Some of this ink was so durable that it has remained legible after 3000 years. It was probably made of lampblack and gum. The ink was mixed with water on a palette when needed.

The pen was made of a reed with softened fibres at one end. These pens were more like narrow paint brushes. (However, Jeremiah speaks of a pen of iron which was used for some writing surfaces (Jer. 17:1). The end of this pen could be sharpened with a knife.

---

*Heaton, *op. cit.,* p. 182.

A certain type of sponge was used for rubbing out errors.

Learning of Trades

A valuable custom of the people was the teaching of some trade or craft to each son. Every Hebrew male had to have a profession or work. Since life was very uncertain and insecure for the Jews, these trades always provided some means of employment. By the time the boys were ten years of age they began to serve at least a part-time apprenticeship. Paul was trained as a Pharisee, yet he had a trade of his own, that of a tent-maker (Acts 18:3).

Aramaic

Hebrew was the language of the Old Testment Scriptures. The language spoken by the Jews of Palestine was Aramaic. In Old Testament times, the land of Aram included parts of Syria and Mesopotamia. It was among these people that this language was first found. Gradually the language of the Arameans spread northward and westward throughout Syria and eventually reached Palestine. Political events caused it to supplant Hebrew in Palestine.

It was the language used by Jesus among His family, friends, and playmates. Some of the writers of the New Testament quote the Aramaic. A few of these Aramaic expressions found in the Gospel of Mark are: "Talitha cumi": "Little girl, I say to you arise" (Mark 5:41); "Ephphatha": "Be opened" (Mark 7:34); and "Eloi, Eloi, lama sabach-thani? . . . My God, my God, why hast thou forsaken me?" (Mark 15:34). The children had to learn two languages: Hebrew, to read the Scriptures, and Aramaic, to converse with each other.

The Torah

The Torah was the name given to the five books of the Pentateuch. They are the first five books of the Old Testament. These were the books of the Mosaic Law which served as the principal text in the synagogue school. Thus with the Torah for their reading book, these children learned to read and write.

The Talmud

For advanced students the Talmud became the important textbook. This book was a large collection of writings, containing a full account of the civil and religious laws of the Jews. It contained the rules and institutions which regulated the life of the Jewish nation. This text explained the duties, beliefs, teachings, and practices of the Hebrew people. It not only contained the teaching of their religion but also the philosophy, medicine, history, judicial proceedings, and practical duties of these people.

The Talmud consisted of two parts: the Mishnah, which is the text, and the Gemara, which is a running commentary. The former deals with the laws, institutions, and rules of life that a Jew must observe. It was written some time during the first or second century A.D. Thus it was not known during the time of Jesus. However, it did serve as a very important part of the education and training of the Jewish people after the destruction of Jerusalem.

The Gemara was a supplement to the Mishnah. It was 15 times as long as the Mishnah. This commentary was arranged in six great divisions, each dealing with some phase of their Hebrew way of life, namely: festivals, the home, the land, worship, defilement, and commerce.

Today the Talmud is very important since it furnishes many hints as to the education of the Hebrew people. It gives us the names of the cities where schools for higher education were found. We are told in the Talmud that Gamaliel had 380 students in his school in Jerusalem. We also learn that Jerusalem had 460 synagogues, each with a meeting place for lectures and the study of the law. The temple had three such meeting places.

BIBLIOGRAPHY

ADAMS, A. McKEE: *Biblical Backgrounds,* Broadman Press, Nashville, Tennessee, 1934.

ALBRIGHT, WILLIAM: *The Archaeology of Palestine and the Bible,* Fleming H. Revell Company, New York, New York, 1935.

BAILEY, ALBERT: *Daily Life in Bible Times,* Charles Scribner's Sons, New York, New York, 1943.

BARTON, GEORGE: *Archaeology and the Bible,* American Sunday School Union, Philadelphia, Pennsylvania, 1916.

BORER, MARY CATHCART: *Two Thousand Years Ago,* Sir Isaac Pitman and Sons, London, England, 1948.

DAY, EDWARD: *The Social Life of the Hebrews,* John C. Nimmo, London, England, 1901.

EAVEY, C. B.: *Principles of Teaching for Christian Teachers,* Zondervan Publishing House, Grand Rapids, Michigan, 1940.

EDERSHEIM, ALFRED: *The Life and Times of the Messiah, Vols. I-II,* E. R. Herrick and Company, New York, New York, 1886.

ELLIS, WILLIAM: *Bible Lands To-day,* D. Appleton and Company, New York, New York, 1927.

ENTWISTLE, MARY: *The Bible Guide Book,* Cokesbury Press, Nashville, Tennessee, 1937.

FALLOWS, SAMUEL: *Bible Encyclopedia,* Howard-Severance Company, Chicago, Illinois, 1911.

FREE, JOSEPH: *Archaeology and the Bible,* Van Kampen Press, Wheaton, Illinois, 1950.

FINNEGAN, JACK: *Light From the Ancient Past,* Princeton University Press, Princeton, New Jersey, 1946.

GETTYS, JOSEPH: *How to Teach the Bible,* John Knox Press, Richmond, Virginia, 1949.

GILL, EMMA: *Home Life in the Bible,* Broadman Press, Nashville, Tennessee, 1936.

GRANT, ELIHU: *The People of Palestine,* J. B. Lippincott Company, Philadelphia, Pennsylvania, 1921.

HEATON, ERIC W.: *Everyday Life in the Old Testament Times,* Charles Scribner's Sons, New York, New York, 1956.

HENDERSON, ARCHIBALD: *Palestine, Its Historical Geography,* T. and T. Clark, Edinburgh, Scotland, 1893.

HOVEY, ALVAH: *The Bible,* The Griffith and Rowland Press, Philadelphia, Pennsylvania.

KELMAN, JOHN: *The Holy Land,* Adam and Charles Black, London, England, 1904

KLINCK, ARTHUR W.: *Home Life in Bible Times,* Concordia Publishing House, St. Louis, Missouri, 1947.

MACKIE, GEORGE: *Bible Manners and Customs,* Fleming H. Revell Company, New York, New York, 1903.

MILLER, MADELEINE AND LANE: *Encyclopedia of Bible Life,* Harper and Brothers Publishers, New York, New York, 1944.

MILLER, RANDOLPH: *The Clue to Christian Education,* Charles Scribner's Sons, New York, New York, 1950.

SCHAFF-HERZOG, *Encyclopedia of Religious Knowledge,* Funk and Wagnalls Company, New York, New York, 1894.

SCHERER, GEORGE: *The Eastern Color of the Bible,* The Sidney Press, Bedford, England.

SMART, JAMES: *The Teaching Ministry of the Church,* Westminster Press, Philadelphia, Pennsylvania, 1954.

SMITH, GEORGE ADAM: *The Historical Geography of the Holy Land,* Harper and Brothers Publishers, New York, New York, 1931.

SMITH, WILLIAM: *A Dictionary of the Bible,* Fleming H. Revell, New York, New York.

THOMSON, W. M.: *The Land and the Book,* Baker Brothers House, Grand Rapids, Michigan, 1954.
The Land and the Book, Vols. I-III, Harper and Brothers, New York, New York, 1886.

WIGHT, FRED H.: *Manners and Customs of Bible Lands,* Moody Press, Chicago, Illinois, 1953.

St Jh. 3:2 — Gordan, Rev
(Radio-announcer)

"We Know that thou art
a Teacher come from
God"

"Jesus a Truly Great Teacher"

Missions
Jamaica
Haiti
Bahamas
Africa